UP-DATE

UP-DATE

Dee W. Hadley

Deseret Book Company   Salt Lake City, Utah   1981

First printing February 1981

Library of Congress Catalog Card No. 81-65308
ISBN 0-87747-847-3

Printed in the United States of America

10   9   8   7   6

To my daughters—
Cheryl Lynn,
Shauneen, Deanne,
and Richelle

Contents

Acknowledgments

Sincere gratitude is expressed to the following persons, without whose help this project would never have been completed: Jacqueline Lambson, Ann Hymus, and Dorothy Tuttle, who provided many hours of typing and moral support; Eleanor Knowles and the editorial and design staffs of Deseret Book, who made excellent contributions; the many students over the years from whom all the date ideas and much of the material on dating have come; and my wife, Audrey, whose sacrifice and patience have made all this possible.

PART 1

IMPROVING YOUR DATING SKILLS

1

Dreaming Won't Make It So

A few months ago a young couple came into my office seeking help for their marriage. They had been married for only six months but said that this was a last attempt at saving a hopeless relationship. They had almost nothing in common. She was from the city; he from the farm. She was a college graduate; he hadn't finished high school. She was religious; he had little interest in religion. And the list went on and on. Why, you ask, did they get married in the first place if they shared so little? The answer, of course, is that they were "in love" and thought love could resolve all their differences.

A second couple had been married a year and a half and had a handsome little boy. The husband had a good job; the wife enjoyed being a homemaker. Every time they talked, however, the discussion ended in an argument. She had spent as many as five days in the hospital after one of his beatings. After two months of counseling, it became obvious that neither of them was willing to change enough to improve the quality of their marriage. They did, however, decide that they were going to "stick it out" because that was "better than divorce." The sad thing about this couple is that if they live an average lifespan, they will have fifty or sixty years of unhappiness together.

Another couple had been married for more than twenty years. They had never been very happy together, and they seldom did things together. He ruled the family with an iron fist and had little consideration for her feelings. She said she had stayed with him only because of the children; now that they were gone, there was no use pretending any more.

I could cite thousands of examples of marriages that haven't been successful. What happens in such marriages that makes them fall apart? When these people married, each one expressed great love for his mate and planned to live happily ever after. Did they change that much after marriage, or did they choose the wrong people to marry? Maybe a more important question is, what are *your* chances of having a marriage like one of these, and what can you do to avoid it?

The statistics are not very encouraging. The divorce rate in the United States in 1978 was reported to be almost fifty percent, up from eight percent at the turn of the century. (*Marriage and Divorce Today*, July 30, 1979, p. 4.) Some sociologists think that of those couples who stay married, only one in ten are really happy. Others say the figure may be as low as one in twenty-five.

If you have some doubt about the number of really happy marriages, look at the couples of your acquaintance. Although you cannot know all about the quality of another person's marriage, how many of them would you like to pattern your marriage after? I hope the number of people you know with good marriages is higher than ten percent, although I have found in asking college students this question that the average is around five percent. In any case, you can see how difficult it is to create a good marriage.

The important question is not how many good marriages there are, but what you have going for you. What makes you think *your* marriage will be better than the ninety percent of marriages that are not what you would want yours to be? Why will *you* succeed where so many have failed?

It takes more than dreams or self-confidence to develop the kind of marriage that puts you in the top ten percent. Yet many young people get caught in one of the worst misjudgments of all: the belief that dreaming about a good marriage will make it happen. In our spectator society, where we learn to watch success without working for it, we come to think our dreams can come true if we do no more than dream. No place is this less true than in marriage, for marriage requires a lot of hard work and maturity for success.

Since there is not enough space here to discuss *all* the causes of a bad marriage or their possible solutions, in this book I would like to focus on one of the major causes of so much unhappiness in marriage: our dating system. It is through dating that you will find the person you are going to marry; dating is also the arena wherein you may practice the interpersonal skills that are so important to a good marriage. Since the four to ten years you spend dating will affect the rest of your life, you will want to make these years most productive.

If, for example, you start dating at age sixteen and marry at twenty-two, and you live the average lifespan of seventy-five years, you have six years to decide how happy or miserable you are going to be for fifty-three years. Making the most of the dating years is essential to your future happiness. But most people, instead of using these years to develop into the kind of person that participates in a successful marriage, just date to have fun and hope they will succeed in marriage. Others spend their time looking for the right one rather than becoming the right one. The dating years should be years of personal growth. This is also the time to develop the interpersonal skills that teach you how to relate to someone else in an intimate relationship.

There are a number of reasons why our dating system doesn't help you develop the skills necessary for a successful marriage or find a mate with whom you can be compatible. Here are eight of the most common:

1. The kinds of dates people go on are much unlike marriage situations, and the parts of a personality you see on a date are nothing like the ones that are important for a good marriage. To coin a phrase, the skills it takes to make a good date are not the skills it takes to be a successful mate. You may be a super skier or dancer, or terrific at holding hands in a movie, and still be lousy at cooking, changing diapers, or budgeting money. Our system does not help you to see each other in ways that give you insight into the kind of mate your date will be.

Two of the worst dates in terms of preparing for marriage are often the most popular ones to go on: going to a movie and going to a dance. Now these are not bad recreational activities, and if you are dating for fun with no thought of getting married, then they are fine. But they contribute little to good mate selection. They rate low because they limit interaction and communication. You don't learn a lot about each other in a movie unless it happens by osmosis while you are holding

5

hands. And much of the dancing done today does not even require a partner, besides which most of the music is so loud that you couldn't communicate even if you wanted to.

2. Most of us grow up with the idea that gratifying our own needs, if not the sole purpose of life, is at least the most important one. As a result, we become "wiifms" (what's in it for me), seeking only self-satisfaction in every experience in a "me" society.

Dating is a basic part of one's self-gratifying experience, an important source of personal entertainment. How many dates have you been on where your only desire was to make your date happy? Oh yes, you wanted to make your partner happy so that he would like you and want to go out with you again, but were you focusing on his needs or your own? How do you decide when a date has been a good one? Usually the answer is, when you have had a good time.

However, dates may also be used for personal growth and for finding an appropriate mate. The problem is that most people date for their personal enjoyment and just happen into marriage. They marry because they "fall in love" with someone they happen to be dating, often with very unhappy results. Dating for personal growth can be fun and is important because it helps you learn a lot about yourself. It also fulfills many of your most important needs, such as the need to be accepted and to feel wanted. Have you ever gone to a dance where all you did was stand by yourself, and no one even talked to you? Or have you gone to a dance where you danced every dance? How does each experience make you feel? If you can remember, then you have learned the value of dating in meeting your need to be accepted.

When people date only to gratify their own needs, they develop what President Spencer W. Kimball has called the most serious problem in marriage—selfishness. When we are able to meet only our own needs, we begin to treat other people as objects. Have you ever been angry and kicked the door or hit the table? Do you feel sorry for the poor door? Of course not, for doors, being objects, do not have feelings. Often we treat others similarly, as if they exist only to make us happy; it doesn't matter if they get hurt, because their feelings are not important to us.

6

3. Another problem is that most people want so badly to be accepted by dates that they try to appear different than they really are. You try to figure out how your date would want you to be and then pretend that you are that kind of person. You learn to play the games that will make others think you have your act together. It's like knocking on your date's door and saying, "Hi, I'm going to play my best games for you tonight; I hope you will approve of them." And so you go out and hide behind your facade, not knowing who you are or with whom you have spent the evening.

The trouble with playing games is that people often act one way before they are married, and afterwards show their true colors. Take, for example, the girl who was the homecoming queen: beautiful, long blonde hair, a great shape, and all that attracts a man. Then she got married. Her long blonde hair became its natural mousy brown shade, and she cut it short and quit taking care of it. She put on fifty pounds and got pimples all over her face. She was just not the same girl that he married. What he got was not what he had planned on.

This phenomenon applies not only to looks, but to personality as well. You have probably heard of the young man who says, "Oh, I'll be super-religious to catch her if that is what she wants." Then when he's got her, he goes back to being his former nonreligious self, and they are both very unhappy about it. You see, what they got was not what they thought they were going to get.

One of the crippling effects of games is their impact on emotional integrity and your sense of self-worth. The more you play games, the less you know about who you really are. If you pretend to have feelings that you don't have or hide the feelings you do have, you get to the point where you are not sure what you really feel or who you are. Many a person in the movie industry has pretended to be someone different than he really is for so long that he has had to go to a psychiatrist to find himself. If you play games for your date and he or she falls in love with the facade and you get married, you have created a dilemma. Do you keep pretending, or do you show your real self? If you don't keep up the facade, your spouse may not like you, so you may decide to keep up the pretense.

When you have lived the lie long enough, you begin to feel unloved, because you know that the person who is loved is not the real you. Your sense of self-worth diminishes.

Because you have worked at playing games and lying to others as well as deceiving yourself, you become less trusting of other people. Often subconsciously you rationalize that if you are lying, they must be lying too; and since they can't be trusted, the whole relationship begins to deteriorate. No good relationship can develop without mutual trust.

Another serious problem with playing games in dating is that you begin to treat the dating process as a game, and as in all games, winning becomes the most important element. You look around and pick out the best prize—the foxiest lady or the macho man—and go after it. The old adage "all's fair in love and war" exemplifies this philosophy: anything you have to do or any game you have to play to catch your prey is okay, because winning the prize is more important than developing an honest, meaningful relationship. You then treat marriage as an arrival rather than a process; it becomes the end of the game rather than the beginning of a long, growing relationship. Hence many people win the dating game and lose the marriage game.

One of the most important tasks in your dating years is to become honest with yourself and to have the courage to show your dates who you really are, without any false impressions or games. Dr. David P. Gardner, president of the University of Utah, was once asked how, as a Mormon, he was able to have such good relations with so many diverse groups. He answered, "You have to decide what your own value system is and always be faithful to it." When you do this, you won't have to remember how you were with a certain person the last time, because you are always the same "you." This is an extremely important principle for success in life as well as in dating. Being the real you is essential if your dates are going to help you prepare for marriage.

4. Dating usually doesn't help one achieve his potential as a person or as a mate, because most people want to get the best there is without paying the price. This may stem from the getting-something-for-nothing attitude in our society. The sports world provides us with a good example. How good a

player do you need to be to play on your church or neighborhood team? How much better would you have to be to make the high school team? How much better than that would you need to be to make the college team? How much better would you need to be to become a professional? The problem is that most of us play at the level of the local church team, but we want the rewards of the pros, and it just can't be done. If you want the rewards of the pros, you have to be willing to pay the price of becoming a pro. Most pros have become great through great personal sacrifice, self-control, and a lot of hard work. An athlete I know, who is on a university swimming team, swims 15,000 yards a day. He works out so hard that he will sometimes sweat under water. Are you willing to work that hard for a good marriage? If you want to have a great marriage, you have to become great. You have to be willing to pay the price required.

Here's a little exercise to help you see the problem. List the traits you would like a mate to have. Then list the traits necessary for you to have in order to catch that person. How many of them do you have?

People seldom marry anyone better than they are. It is like the old story of the young lady who baked a cherry pie that turned out rather badly—so badly, in fact, that she couldn't feed it to her husband on a plate. She had to put it in a cereal bowl and he had to use a spoon rather than a fork to eat it. Halfway through the pie, he paused and said, "Hey, I've got to tell you how bad this pie really is," as though she were too dumb to notice all by herself. He then continued, "And while I'm at it, let me tell you about some other things I see wrong with you." He then listed four or five of her less-than-sterling qualities. She replied, "Hold it! I'm completely aware of those things. Those are the things that prevented me from getting a better husband than you!" The lesson: You need to make yourself the best self you can possibly become to get the best mate you possibly can.

You also need to recognize that finding a mate is a competitive experience, and that the best people go out with only top-quality people. I remember one extremely attractive young woman who came into my office. I thought to myself that she really should not have any trouble getting dates. That was true. She got all the dates she wanted, but not with the young men she would have chosen. None of those with whom she wanted to go asked her out. I said, "Well, the thing you want to do is get into the top ten percent of the young women. Although you are attractive enough to compete with them, maybe you ought to look at yourself and see what traits you could develop that would make you more attractive in other respects. All of the girls you are competing with are physically attractive, but the best boys are only going to date the best girls. If you want to be successful in dating, you need to improve your total self, not just your looks." Perhaps the greatest thing you can do in your dating years is to become the very best person you can and pay the price necessary to find the best mate for the best marriage.

5. Perhaps the biggest problem with our dating system is our belief that it will lead to an emotional experience we call love, and then you will marry the person you are "in love" with and live happily ever after. This idea that "love can conquer all" may not bring you as much success as you expect.

A student from India who studied in America wrote of the differences in our cultures: "You fall in love and get married; we get married and then fall in love." The system in his country, where love is not one of the important factors in choosing a mate, seems to work as well as, if not better than, our system based on love.

A contemporary song claims that "Love will keep us together." Being confronted with this concept day in and day out, it is no wonder young people think that love can overcome any problem, that it has the power to cure all the ills of life. But love rarely overcomes differences in religion, culture, personality, values, expectations, or family background. In fact, differences in areas such as these, over some time, may destroy any love that does exist between two people. The shortest marriage I have seen in which the couple thought they were in love lasted a week and a half. After that time, they couldn't stand each other.

Maybe one of our problems is that love is so hard to define. How do you know when you are in love, and if it is the kind of love that will last a lifetime? In tennis love means nothing, but in marriage it can mean almost anything. If you were to read one hundred books on love, you would probably get one hundred different definitions of love. If a banana could talk back to a man who said he loved bananas, it might say, "What do you mean you love me? All you want to do is peel me, take the best out of me, and throw the rest away." Is there a difference when I say I love my wife, I love my children, and I love sports cars? I use the same verb. Do I mean the same thing? If these concepts are different, what is the difference? Your own definition will be the most important to your marriage. You need to decide how you should treat those you love and how they should act if they love you. There should be agreement between you and your beloved, because love isn't love unless it is expressed in actions.

Understanding love is difficult, and most of us have had so little experience with love that we probably aren't sure what the emotion should be like. So perhaps instead of counting for eighty or ninety percent of the reason for picking a mate, it ought to count for only twenty to twenty-five percent.

6. Related to love is another problem in the mate-selection process: the emphasis we put on good looks. Good looks can be both a blessing and a curse. They are a blessing because good-looking people are usually the most popular and they get more dates. They also find it easier to succeed in school and to get jobs than unattractive people do, especially if the unattractive one is also overweight.

Good looks can also be a disadvantage. People charmed by good looks may overlook other qualities that could be detrimental to a good marriage. They may treat a good-looking person as an object, a trophy to be won. Because of their popularity, good-looking people do not always take time to learn the interpersonal skills necessary for successful marriage.

7. A General Authority who has performed hundreds of marriage ceremonies has kept track of the length of time the couples had known each other from their first date to their marriage. The average time was five and one-half months. The amount of time people spend together and the quality of that time has a tremendous effect on their marriage.

When people spend time together, they develop patterns of behavior that make the relationship predictable and rewarding. The longer a relationship exists before marriage, the more natural and genuine the behavior patterns become and the better the marriage should be, if those involved are not playing games, which could develop destructive false patterns. A year or two of honest courtship, then, should make a better marriage than a six-month courtship.

Not only is the amount of time you spend dating important, but also the quality of the dates. I indicated earlier the two worst kinds of dates, but there is more involved than just that. If you were dating someone who had seen *Star Wars* sixty-six times, you probably would know only one part of that person's personality. Nor will you learn a lot of helpful information if you see a person only once a month for two years. Every night for six weeks won't do it either, even if you are sure you are in love. To be successful, you need a variety of dates that show as many aspects of your personality as possible. You also need to see each other at a variety of times, at both different times of day and different times of the week.

8. Another problem with our dating system is that we do not date enough different people to know which one will be most suitable for us.

A young couple started going steady in the ninth grade and neither ever dated anyone else. Two days after their high school graduation, they got married. After five years of marriage, they moved from their small farming community to a big city. She took a job to help support the two children and learned from the women at work that most husbands don't lose their tempers every time the wife does not perform as expected. She began to find men who treated her with kindness, and she soon became unhappy with her marriage. If during her dating years she had looked around a while and known what kind of personality was most suited to her, she might not have run into her later problems. You need to be acquainted with enough different personalities to see which one seems to be most compatible with your own.

There are a couple of cautions I would offer to those playing the field. First, when you date a lot of people, you often come to expect to find a mate who is an accumulation of all of the best qualities of all of the people you have dated, while possessing none of their negative qualities. Thus, people create unrealistic expectations about what a marriage relationship should be. Since we are imperfect, we need to recognize that other people are imperfect too, and, in fact, we need to see their imperfections as a source of strength in the relationship.

Second, sometimes a person's personality is such that he can be emotionally involved with only one person at a time. (Sometimes these people fall in love with everyone they date.) Therefore, he usually dates fewer people than do those who can maintain a relationship with several people. You should take some time to find out which type you are, because the first group needs to be more careful than the second in selecting dates.

2

A Time to Play the Field

Not all people are equally successful in dating. Sometimes the best-looking people don't get the most or the best dates. Many people go through the dating years and are totally unprepared for marriage, or they choose someone who is entirely wrong for them. Often these difficulties arise because people don't go through all the stages of dating in their proper order, or they don't stay in a stage long enough to develop the skills that should be learned during that stage.

It takes time to develop the skills needed to be a useful, happy adult. Some people want to grow up so quickly that they stunt their emotional growth. The stages-of-dating concept is designed to help you grow up in the most productive way. The following chart will help you to see this concept:

Know Thyself	Group Dating	Playing the Field
12-14	14-16	16-18
Going Steady	Engaged	Married
18-20	20+	21+

If you are older and have missed some of the stages, you still need to learn the skills that are important to those stages of life. Older people will not need to spend quite as much time in each stage. Teenagers ought to spend at least a year or two in each stage; older persons may get by with six months to a year.

Let's look at each of these stages briefly to see why they are important.

14

Know Thyself

After you reach puberty (you can always tell when that is—the boys start taking showers and combing their hair and girls worry about what they wear and how they smell), you become aware of members of the opposite sex and you want to impress them. However, you won't be very successful if you don't have some understanding of who you are.

A student once asked me why he was never able to get a second date with a girl after he had taken her out once. As we explored his personality, it became clear that he had some traits that might be offensive to girls. The trouble was that he had not recognized these traits. Because he was unaware of himself and the impact he had on other people, he was labeled a real "dud" on a date.

Self-awareness is not only the first prerequisite to successful dating, but it also relates directly to the degree of happiness you experience the rest of your life. Understanding yourself is a lifetime project; you may never have complete self-understanding, but at least you need to be working on it, to practice getting in touch with your real feelings and with who you really are. You don't need to give in to all of your feelings, but you do need to know they exist.

Group Dating

As you get to know yourself, you also need to spend some time getting to understand the opposite sex. Men and women do not think alike on many issues. I have found that many of the difficulties in marriage stem from the differences between men and women. Often a man will think he has a strange wife when she is really just acting like most women.

An example may help illustrate this. When does your mother start getting ready for Christmas? If she is like most women, it is about the first of October. Now, when does your father start getting ready for Christmas? On December 24, right? Or maybe December 23. This doesn't mean that one method is less desirable than the other. It's just that for most women the planning stage of an activity is as rewarding as the execution stage. Have you noticed that when there is a girl's-choice dance, the girls generally ask much earlier than boys would for a boy's-choice dance?

15

In your dating experience you need to have some time when you learn to understand and deal with the opposite sex. This can be done best where there are groups of boys and girls interacting, where there isn't much need for the self-protection that often accompanies one-on-one dating. School, church, or community youth activities where there isn't such pressure to succeed are the kinds of things you should be involved in during the group stage.

A person who misses this group-dating stage may spend a great deal of time during his marriage trying to understand or trying to make his mate into the person he wishes that person would be. This doesn't usually work very well.

Playing the Field
Not only do you need to learn that men and women generally don't think alike, but also that each person is unique. John doesn't think like Jim or Joe or Jerry. Mary has quite different interests from Melissa or Meg or Marta. Playing the field gives you a chance to check out several different kinds of people so you can decide what kind of personality and life-style best suits you. It is surprising how many people do not take the time to find out who suits them best until after they get married, and then they may find that they are not very compatible with their mates.

This stage may be the most important stage of dating, because it is here that you learn so much about yourself. It is helpful to see yourself through the eyes of several different people.

Going Steady
After you have dated enough people, going steady is a good experience. There is some evidence that those who have gone steady two or three times have a better chance at succeeding in marriage than those who have never gone steady. This tends to be true because in this stage, you have to learn the give-and-take of a close interpersonal relationship. You also have to learn those problem-solving techniques that are so vital to a good marriage.

Engagement

For most people, this is just a time to get ready for the wedding. Although preparing for the wedding is important, a couple should also use this time to get to know each other in greater depth and solve as many potential problems as possible. It is surprising how much you can learn once you have committed yourself to another person.

Marriage

Now, if your dating has been all that it should be, you take that leap of faith (for that is what marriage is) that brings you to a partnership with another person. Then the hard and most rewarding work of life begins.

3
How Well Do You Like Yourself?

Since you probably won't marry anyone better than you are, dating should be a time when you work on making yourself the kind of person who will be a good marriage partner. Instead of trying to act like Cal Cool or Patty Perfect on every date, you should be using many of your dates to assist you in your personal growth. Try being a better you; then if you bomb on a date, chalk it up to experience—a chance to learn and grow. There are eleven areas of personal growth that are important to work on while dating. They are:

1. Developing self-esteem
2. Becoming emotionally mature
3. Developing a pleasing personality
4. Understanding and dealing with your sexual feelings
5. Developing a workable value system
6. Developing a meaningful life-style
7. Learning to relate to others
8. Developing good social skills
9. Learning to communicate
10. Learning to understand love
11. Learning how to get a date

These areas will be discussed in the remainder of Part I, starting with self-esteem in this chapter.

Self-confidence is perhaps the most important ingredient in successful dating. When you feel good about yourself, it is reflected in others' attitudes toward you. If a date goes badly, a person with high self-esteem will say, "That one didn't turn out well; I guess I'll have to work on doing better." A person with low self-esteem might say, "I knew I was a dud and she wouldn't like me; I might as well forget the whole thing."

A person who doesn't develop a real sense of self-worth

will usually fake one, because he wants others to think he is good even if he doesn't think so himself. You have probably seen people try to fake a good sense of self-worth. Some of them are:

"The Know-It-All," who always has to be right. He has to win every argument.

"The Bully," who always has to be in charge and who pushes others around to get his own way.

"The Shy Guy," who never seems to get involved.

"The Liar," who tells stories to play himself down so others will build him up.

"The Briber," who is always giving things away to be liked.

"The Rich Man," who thinks that driving the latest sports car and wearing the newest fashions will make people like him.

"The Fisher," who depends on the approval of others for his self-esteem.

"The Give-Inner," who allows others to make his decisions for him. He always goes along even if he thinks it is wrong.

"The Daydreamer," who spends his time in a fantasy world. He may live too much in the past or too much in the future.

"The Status Seeker," who belongs to the "right group" or drives the "right car" or dates the "right people."

And the list could go on. However, it is important to know that none of these people really like themselves. They use these techniques to make you think that they are okay.

If you are immature and inexperienced, you may confuse a temporary feeling of achievement with a genuine sense of self-worth. Such false feelings often come when you have "conquered" a date and made him submissive to your will or when you have dated someone who gives you social status. This might happen when you get that date with the homecoming queen, the cheerleader, the captain of the football team, or the student body president.

People who are not sure of their self-esteem often spend the time on their dates and even in their married life trying to get others to build up their own sense of self-worth. However, the people who are most successful in dating and marriage are those who genuinely love themselves, who can forget their own needs and focus on making others happy. People who like themselves have a quiet self-assurance. They don't have to spend time showing off or having others tell them how good they are.

Since self-esteem is probably the most important quality of successful people in life, in dating, and in marriage, we would like to suggest some things that can help you develop a sense of self-worth during your dating days. Although your dating experience isn't going to change a really poor sense of self-worth that has been developed in an adverse family environment, it can be a place to learn to like yourself more.

The first step in developing a sense of self-worth is being honest with yourself and with others. We mentioned earlier the problem of playing games and their effect on your sense of self-worth. When other people like what they see in you—and when what they see is really you—you will begin to like yourself more. You'll get more dates too.

It is important to your sense of self-worth that you live by those values that are important to you and respect your dates' rights to live by their value systems. If you change your values for the approval of others, you will soon learn to dislike yourself. Many young people lower their standards in hopes that by so doing they will be loved, only to find that they are no happier than before, and that self-hate has perhaps crept in. It is always destructive to self-esteem to live for the approval of others. If you spend all the time on dates trying to be what you think others want you to be, your values and your self-worth will suffer. If you act on your date so that you are proud of yourself, and if you treat your partners so that they will like themselves as well when the date is over, your sense of self-worth will continue to grow.

Don't expect perfection from yourself on dates. If you expect every date to come out exactly right, you will be cheating yourself out of a chance to grow. Sometimes the dates that prepare you best for a happy life are the ones that seem disastrous at the time.

You have probably heard of or maybe even attended one of the positive-thinking seminars that are so popular these

days. They teach one of the great principles of life and especially of dating: No one likes the person who is always negative. When you get home after a date with a negative person,
you really feel depressed. The most popular people are those
who like themselves and are enthusiastic about the things
they are doing. In fact, some studies show that being enthusiastic about life and acting positively are more important to
successful dating than good looks.

To become more positive, you can learn to think nice
things about yourself and avoid dwelling on your mistakes.
People who are always bragging are really fishers who need
others to convince them that they are okay. But when you
think well of yourself, you don't need to brag, because you
show self-confidence, which will cause others to have confidence in you.

I have a friend who works at a detention center. He said
that at first he would come home so depressed that it was beginning to affect his family life. He decided to do something to
change his attitude. He would get up in the morning and look
in the mirror and say,"You are good. You can do it. Life is
great; you can go help those kids." When he did this, he could
go through the day feeling good about himself. Try this and
see if you like yourself more. No one wants to spend a whole
date listening to your troubles. Learn and grow from your
mistakes; don't spend all your time worrying about them.
Forget them and move on to new challenges.

Develop a sense of humor. People who enjoy life and find
it exciting are always fun to date. People who can laugh at
themselves seem to get the most from life.

To develop self-esteem, you need to be responsible for
your own life. You need to own your feelings. If you are happy or sad, it is because you choose to be. No one is forcing you
to feel the way you do. All of us, except those whose freedom
has been taken away or who are handicapped, are exactly
who we want to be. So if your dates are not fun or you're not
getting any dates, you can choose to do something about it.

When you come home from a date that you did not particularly enjoy, do you blame it on the person you were with or
do you accept the responsibility? Of course, if it is your date's
fault that you didn't have a good time, then you don't have to

worry about trying to improve yourself. Once you accept responsibility for your own feelings and the success or failure of your dates, not only will you have more dates, but you will enjoy them more as well. There is a great deal of difference between being aware of and responsible for the impact of your behavior on others and letting others decide what kind of person you will be. The first is essential for a self-loving person while the latter is a trait of those who have low self-esteem.

Responsible people also know that complaining doesn't change things very much. If you are moody because the weather is bad or your math teacher doesn't like you very much, or because the best-looking person on the block does not want to go out with you, the only one you will make miserable is yourself. It doesn't seem profitable to continue to hurt yourself. You will be way ahead of the game if you are enthusiastic about your life.

You'll like yourself better and you'll have more dates if you are active, involved, and achieving. If you are genuinely involved in school and church activities, your chances for developing the kind of character that will make for a good date and a good marriage will be greatly enhanced. If you are active in sports, drama, dance, or music, you can develop a better sense of self-worth.

You will be a better date if you do your best in school or at work or even at home. People who strive for excellence are always the most marriageable people. They work to succeed in everything they do. They work hard, study hard, and play hard. They also don't give up when things go badly. You will recall that Thomas Edison failed hundreds of times before he invented the incandescent light; Henry Ford was penniless at forty; Albert Einstein flunked math—but they each persisted anyway. Success in dating requires the same kind of persistence. People who like themselves learn to recover quickly from their failures.

Socrates said, "Know thyself." That may be the most important task you have in life—and it may take a lifetime to achieve. You can't start too soon, and dating gives you an excellent chance to begin to grow.

4

What Do You Want to Be When You Grow Up?

The most mature people are those who deal most constructively with their own feelings and with the world around them. No one is mature all of the time, no matter what his age. Depending on the circumstances, everyone does things that are really immature at times.

William C. Menninger states: "No one can go through life without being under tension at one time or another. All of us experience anxious moments about a situation or a problem. We all get panicky over uneasy feelings and often are unable to face our problems objectively. But the more mature we are, the better we will understand these feelings. We will know that at times we will become confused and may behave in unreasonable ways. Our maturity depends, to a certain extent, on how well we can handle our problems and how easily we can turn the tenseness that often accompanies problems into productive outlets." (*Growing Up Emotionally* [Chicago: Science Research Associates, 1957], p. 21.)

If your friends try to make you think that they are always in control, they are probably acting out of a sense of insecurity. Successful people are often the most willing to reveal their neuroses. The first task in becoming honest with yourself is to learn to admit, at least to yourself, your strengths and weaknesses. It is as important to be in tune with your strengths as it is to understand your weaknesses.

One problem is that too often people tend to show their most immature behavior around those whom they would most like to impress. Have you noticed that when you go out with persons you don't really care about, you are more relaxed and they usually want to go out with you again? But when you go out with someone you really care about, you are often uptight and you blow the whole thing. If you relax and try to be your real self, you will probably be more successful.

During your dating experience you need to work on your maturity, because the most mature people are generally the ones who get the most dates, and then are also the ones who have the best marriages.

Check the following traits of a mature person and start working on the ones you feel you need to improve.

Self-Confidence

Immature people are afraid of being rejected; they deal very poorly with criticism and are always trying to live up to the expectations of others. In dating they become overly competitive, dominate the conversation, or make all the decisions. They become possessive and expect others to do what they want them to. They often act superior, cocky, or snobbish. They become perfectionists, overly self-critical, never showing their weaknesses or allowing themselves to be happy or satisfied.

Optimism

Immature people spend a lot of time looking at the negative side of life. They are often prophets of doom. They seldom enjoy life; many of them don't believe that life should be enjoyed. They spend a lot of time finding fault or belittling other people in order to build themselves up.

Mature people are basically happy, positive individuals who generally anticipate success. They are usually pleased with the world around them.

Postponement of Gratification

Have you noticed that children will usually choose an immediate reward instead of waiting for something better? Have you also noticed that many adults also want immediate gratification of their personal needs without much thought of the long-term effect? They have unpredictable and inconsistent behavior.

Mature people trust their judgment and won't sacrifice their values for the approval of others. They are not destroyed by the hostility or disapproval of others. They are willing to let others share the stage with them. They have the ability to let others win some of the time and don't need always to be in control. They are willing to accept and admit both their strengths and their weaknesses.

Self-Control

Children are impulsive. They want to gratify their own needs without considering the effect on others. They are only concerned about the effects of a situation on their personal comfort. Children tend to be self-indulgent and don't like to share. They often show a low tolerance for frustration.

Mature people do not deny their feelings, but they learn to express them in ways that are not destructive to themselves or others. They are not unduly overwhelmed or overly distressed by uncertainty. They learn to handle new and unexpected situations with a minimum of emotional discomfort.

Realism

Those who are immature live by their emotions. They determine how they should live and what is right and wrong strictly by their feelings. They live a lot of their lives in a world of daydreams and make-believe, often escaping an unpleasant world by retreating into movies, television, or books. They spend a lot of time wishing the world were different from what it is. They live mostly in the past or the future.

Mature people do not let their emotions overwhelm them, but are guided by the facts and realities of life. They dream about a better life but are content to enjoy life as it is. They are not overly upset when life isn't all that they want it to be. They learn to live with that part of life they can't change.

Mature people are able to choose more wisely and are willing to postpone present gratification for their future well-being or the well-being of their loved ones. Patience is one of their outstanding virtues.

Responsibility

Immature people tend to be defensive. When things go wrong either with their environment or with themselves, they tend to blame others. They are usually irresponsible. They might be slow to start projects that need to be accomplished, or they fail to finish projects, or at least they wait until the last

25

minute to accomplish the task. They cannot take criticism well; they feel that they must justify themselves; they tend to protect themselves.

Mature people accept the responsibility for their own behavior and the behavior of dependent people. They accept the responsibility for the effect of their behavior on others but do not allow others' opinions to determine their behavior. They have learned to accept criticism without being defensive.

Adaptability

Having to be right all of the time is one of the signs of immature people. They find it hard to admit they are wrong. They are often so rigid that they find it difficult to listen to or accept points of view that are new or different from their own.

Mature people know that the world is not always going to be what they want it to be, so they learn to change their expectations or their plans. They adapt to new situations with a minimum amount of trauma. Adaptability is probably one of the most important guidelines of a successful marriage. The adaptable or flexible person is willing to be tentative in his judgment about the world and about people.

Commitment

Immature people shift their values, their friends, or their story to fit the changing situation. Their inconsistency makes it difficult to predict their behavior. They are often nonconformists who feel a need to rebel. They want to get the maximum amount of benefit with the minimum amount of effort. They feel they should do less and get more than others. They are usually not very dependable.

Mature people, on the other hand, have values that are strong and long-lasting, and they are affected very little by the changing situation. They use their time wisely. When they work, they work hard. When they play, they play hard. Their consistency makes them dependable. Once committed, they can be counted on to follow through. Being dependable and consistent is important if you want to succeed in dating.

Relating Well to Other People

Mature people have good relationships with other people.

26

WHAT DO YOU WANT TO BE WHEN YOU GROW UP?
They are concerned about others' feelings. This is such an important part of dating and maturity that we will discuss it in a separate section.

5

Ponder Your Personality

A few years ago an attractive single woman in her middle thirties came into my office. She wanted to know why she had never married and what she could do to catch a man. Like many attractive people, she thought her good looks were enough to get her a husband. What she had to learn was that personality is far more important in successful dating than good looks. Many of the important traits she should have learned at age sixteen and seventeen she had missed because her looks had gotten her by. But attraction based solely on looks seldom makes for a lasting relationship.

A young, extremely beautiful woman I know who has been married three times will probably go through two or three more marriages because she is not willing to develop the kind of personality necessary to be happy in a marriage.

Before we talk about the kind of personality that good dating ought to develop, let's examine who you are. Fill out the Personality Inventory Chart 1 (page 29). In column 1 of the chart, put a check beside each of the ten characteristics that best describe who you are. In column 2 check the ten characteristics that are least descriptive of who you are.

Since you can't always see yourself clearly, it might be helpful to have two or three people who know you well fill out the inventory for you. Don't trust their conclusions as being the absolute right answer, but use them as additional information to help you in your quest for self-understanding.

When you have completed that chart, fill out the Personal Inventory Chart 2 (page 29). In column 1, again check the ten traits that best describe you, and in column 2 check the ten least descriptive traits.

Now, with this information you can begin to look at the areas of your personality that might need to be improved.

Personal Inventory Chart 1

	1	2		1	2		1	2
Accepting			Even-tempered		X	Responsible		
Adaptable			Enthusiastic	X		Self-controlled		
Adventurous	X		Expects to be treated kindly			Self-confident		
Affectionate		X	Forgiving			Self-respecting		
Appreciative			Frank, forthright		X	Sense of duty		
Beautiful			Fun-loving			Sense of humor	X	
Big-hearted			Genuine	X		Sensitive to others		X
Careful about appearance			Gives praise readily			Sentimental		
Careful about money			Good listener			Shares feelings easily		X
Calm			Hard worker			Sociable		
Charitable			Helpful			Spiritual		
Compassionate			Honest			Sympathetic		
Committed			Likes to make others happy			Tactful		X
Companionable			Methodical worker		X	Tender		
Concerned about feelings of others			Neat, orderly		X	Thoughtful		
Cooperative			Obedient			Trusting		
Courteous			Optimistic	X		Trustworthy		
Creative	X		Out-going	X		Understanding	X	
Dependable			Pays attention to detail			Varied interests		
Easy-going	X		Positive			Well-mannered		
Efficient			Respects the rights of others			Willing worker		
Encouraging						Willing to accept a subordinate role		

Personal Inventory Chart 2

	1	2		1	2		1	2
Afraid			Closed			Conceited		
Angry			Competitive in social situations			Critical of others		
Anxious for approval			Complains too much			Daydreamer		
Argumentative	X					Demanding		
						Dependent		

29

	1	2		1	2		1	2
Depressed			Inflexible		X	Procrastinates	X	X
Dictatorial			Intolerant			Puts others down		
Distant			Irritable			Radical		X
Dogmatic			Jealous			Rebellious		X
Domineering			Lazy			Resentful		
Easily discouraged		X	Loud			Sarcastic		
Easily excited	X		Moody		X	Sassy, talks back		
Easily hurt			Nagging			Self-centered		
Easily swayed		X	Narrow-minded		X	Self-indulgent		X
Extravagant		X	Needs lots of praise			Shrewd, devious		
Feels inferior			Nervous			Shy		
Gossips indiscreetly			Overly aggressive			Stubborn		X
Hostile			Overly neat			Submissive		
Impatient			Overly talkative		X	Teasing		X
Impractical			Overly trusting			Touchy		
Impulsive		X	Pessimistic			Uncommunicative		X
Inconsiderate			Phony		X	Uninvolved		
			Possessive					

It would help if you were to have one of your parents (the one who would be the most candid) and one or two good friends fill these traits out for you. Be sure you don't take their word as the absolute truth, because no one really knows you, not even yourself. But with this information, you can begin to look at the areas of your personality that need to be improved.

It's important to know that you don't need to stay the way you are. You can change! Dating ought to provide you with the chance to try on some new personality traits. Try being pleasant and self-assured. Remember, you don't always have to be in control of every situation, or, conversely, you might try being a little more assertive on your next date. You might also try practicing some of these positive traits on family members. Be nice to them even when you don't feel they deserve it. If you wait until you are married to try to develop the kind of personality it takes to make a good marriage, it will be too late. The few years of teens and early twenties determine to a large extent how successful you'll be the rest of your life.

To help you see what other people who are dating look for in a date, we asked two hundred students who attend the Salt Lake Institute of Religion adjacent to the University of Utah to list the five things they liked and the five things they disliked in a date. (See lists below.) Although the number one choice reflected the religious background of our sample, the rest seemed fairly consistent with other surveys. Pick out those traits in which you seem to be deficient and start working on improving them. (Responses are scored on a scale of 1 to 10.)

GIRLS

What traits cause you to want a first date with a boy?

Religious, honors priesthood	9.40
Respects me, treats me like a lady	9.23
Easy to talk to	9.10
Makes me feel at ease	8.98
Responsible	8.98
Wants to be with me	8.83
Well mannered	8.82
Courteous	8.76
Friendly	8.67
Likes his family	8.57
Enjoys being with people	8.56
Honest	8.52
Polite	8.44
Self-confident	8.43
Positive	8.42
Communicates well	8.36
Caring	8.35
Interested in me	8.35
Good grooming	8.34
Sense of humor	8.33

BOYS

What traits do you look for in a first date?

Good shape	9.13
Outgoing, friendly	8.85
Positive, happy, enthusiastic	8.85
Clean	8.72
Testimony	8.64
Good looks	8.56
Easy to talk to, pleasant	8.38
Honest	8.31
Religious	8.14
Dresses neatly, modestly	8.11
Interested in me	8.11
Open and honest	8.04
Intelligent	7.92
Self-confident	7.65
Hair well kept	7.58
Self-respecting	7.28
Similar values	7.21
Similar interests	7.18
Sense of humor, witty	7.13
Even disposition	7.13

31

GIRLS		BOYS	
What traits cause you to turn down a first date?		What traits cause you not to ask a girl for a first date?	
Bad language	9.13	Smokes	9.94
Crude jokes	9.02	Smells	9.64
Doesn't honor his priesthood	8.96	Dresses poorly, poor taste in clothes	9.46
Treats a girl like an object	8.80	Ugly	9.38
		Acts too good for me	9.34
Too aggressive	8.64	Fat	9.09
Bad temper	8.62	Swears	9.07
Not honest	8.60	Poor appearance	9.02
Not religious	8.58	Phony	8.95
Puts people down	8.51	Bad manners	8.87
Not kind to his family	8.51	Stuck up	8.74
Insincere	8.50	Poor personal hygiene	8.72
Comes on too strong	8.29	Fake	8.49
Negative attitude	8.25	Only interested in herself	8.40
Doesn't know how to treat a lady	8.22	Poor language	8.24
		Not religious	8.12
Greasy hair, pimples, skinny	8.08	Boisterous	8.09
Conceited	8.04	Won't talk	8.04
Too pushy	8.00	Self-centered	8.00
Too serious	7.99	Puts others down	8.00
Poor manners	7.87		
No goals	7.86		

After 3 or 4 dates, what traits cause you to continue to date a boy?		After you have dated a girl 3 or 4 times what causes you to continue to ask her out?	
Honors priesthood	9.76	Great potential as a mother	9.72
I feel I am better for being with him	9.51	Good moral standards, views	9.26
Good communication	9.50	Good communication	9.16
Honest	9.44	Cares for the relationship	9.09
Personalities match	9.40	Good values	9.08
Spiritual	9.26		
Respects me	9.25		

GIRLS		BOYS	
Can get beyond a shallow conversation	9.18	Able to be herself	8.99
Easy to talk to	9.13	Doesn't give you the cold shoulder	8.96
Happy	9.11	Able to play and enjoy each other	8.94
Testimony	9.09		
Makes me feel special	9.06	Shows she cares	8.93
Self-respect	9.02	Ability to bring out the good in me	8.93
Stable and happy about life	9.01	Sensitive about others' feelings	8.84
Spiritually mature but not self-righteous	8.97	Good Church member, has testimony	8.76
Good personal hygiene	8.97	Spiritual	8.66
Potentially good husband	8.96	Makes me feel special	8.64
Mutual interests	8.92	Mature	8.60
Sense of humor and sensitive	8.86	True interest in my feelings	8.60
Fun to be with	8.82	I feel good about being with her	8.59
		Common interests	8.54
		Good sense of humor	8.53
		Benefits me spiritually	8.42

After 3 or 4 dates, what traits cause you to not continue to date a boy?		After you have dated a girl 3 or 4 times, what traits cause you to quit asking her out?	
Rude	9.63	Vulgar	9.00
Uses me	9.51	Dishonest	8.96
Poor communication	9.48	Constantly breaking dates	8.61
Tells my secrets to his friends	9.34	Selfish	8.67
Foul language	9.31	Phony excuses	8.54
Too much physical expression without really caring	9.30	Thinks she's God's gift	8.53
		Cold	8.38

33

GIRLS		BOYS	
Has bad habits	9.30	Always complaining	8.38
Talks about other		Too serious	8.36
dates	9.27	Acts bored	8.29
Doesn't honor his		Overweight	8.24
priesthood	9.22	"Dingy," "spacy"	8.21
Too aggressive	8.80	Negative	8.07
Unwilling to change	8.77	Shallow personality	8.05
Plays games	8.75	No emotional	
Conceited	8.68	feedback	8.05
Critical of others	8.64	Clams up, afraid to	
Doesn't let me express		relax	8.01
myself	8.60	No sense of humor	8.00
Not appreciative	8.57	No potential as a good	
Only thinks of himself	8.52	mother	7.99
Jealous, suspicious	8.49	Selfish, demanding	7.96
Not "up-front"	8.46	Different values	7.94
Too possessive	8.38		

6

A Wonderful Servant—a Terrible Master

Sexual feelings and attraction to the opposite sex come to almost all people when they reach puberty. Having these feelings does not guarantee that you will know how to use them to your best advantage. You need to develop a philosophy of sex that will help you make it a meaningful part of the rest of your life. Such a philosophy is well expressed by two noted religious leaders.

Joseph F. Smith once said that sex was not only for having children, "but for the development of the higher faculties and nobler traits of human nature, which the love-inspired companionship of man and woman alone can insure."

Billy Graham stated this same concept: "The Bible celebrates sex and its proper use, presenting it as God-created, God-ordained, God-blessed. It makes plain that God himself implanted the physical magnetism between the sexes for two reasons: for the propagation of the human race, and for the expression of that kind of love between man and wife that makes for true oneness.... It teaches clearly that sex can be a wonderful servant but a terrible master: that it can be a creative force more powerful than any other in the fostering of a love, companionship, happiness or can be the most destructive of all of life's forces." ("What the Bible Says About Sex," *Reader's Digest*, May 1970, p. 118.)

In our society we do not learn to connect sexual feelings with deep relationships because sexual feelings are so often exploited for commercial gain. Some people use sex to get power or wealth; others use it to manipulate, control, pay off, or reward. Sexual feelings can respond to a lot of stimuli that have nothing to do with a close relationship. Therefore, when people marry, they often don't know how to connect their sexual feelings with their love for their mates.

There are those who use sex to hide their insecurity or feelings of low self-esteem, to "prove" they are popular, to make them feel "in" with the gang, to "prove" they are grown up or that they "love" one another, or to make their partners feel committed, none of which are mature uses of this powerful emotion. Sometimes young people will spend their dating time necking, and will avoid areas of disagreement that in a healthy dating relationship would have shed some light on their potential for a good marriage. Often when they can't solve a problem or they are having a fight, they think that if they kiss and make up, the problem will go away. I know of one couple who used this technique for twenty years before they realized it didn't work; the resulting divorce was a tragedy for both partners and their six children. Sex is often used as a cover-up for poor communication, but it never works. Too often sexual activity gets in the way of quality communication or becomes a substitute for communication skills.

Probably the greatest tragedy produced by the commercialization of sex is that people may learn to treat it as a self-indulgent experience. In the movies, its only purpose is to gratify one's own needs or to be used to manipulate someone else. Sex becomes a matter of conquest rather than fulfillment. Often the other person becomes an object whose only purpose is to make you look good, to indulge your passions, to make you feel secure, or even to help you become popular. Because sex at its worst can still seem rewarding, you are often willing to settle for less than the best, to accept less than you deserve.

You kiss your date goodnight and he or she says, "Wow, did that feel good! Let's do it again." What he or she is saying is, "Please let me use you to gratify my needs." When you do this, on a scale from one to ten the best you can hope for is a five, because that is all you can give from a self-indulgent approach to sex. If you want to develop the higher faculties and nobler traits that put you at ten, you have to begin to use your physical relations to say something different. You need to be saying, "I respect you, I cherish you, I honor you, I love you, and this is my way of telling you." If what you want to do is honor, cherish, love, and respect someone, then you would never do anything that is inappropriate, nor would you want your companion to go farther than intended, to lower standards or values just to appease your appetite. Nor would you use sex to overcome your own inadequacies, to repair a faltering ego, to be liked, to hide your insecurities, or to bolster up a failing relationship.

Because this area of a relationship is so personally rewarding, and because it is so easy to learn, people have a tendency to move faster in this area than in the other important areas, until it begins to monopolize the relationship. How long do you think it would take to learn to kiss well? Maybe two minutes if you are a slow learner. Now, how much longer will it take you to understand how another person sees the world? If you are really good at it, maybe a year. Yet understanding this is as important to a good marriage as is sex. However, most people follow the line of least resistance, and this clouds the rest of the relationship.

Premarital sexual activity usually results in a deterioration of the relationship. It makes the building of a relationship difficult, because it becomes a substitute for solving problems and developing good communication skills. It also hurts the relationship in other ways. Sexual activity almost always causes a breakdown in trust and respect. If your partner is using you, then you can't be sure that he or she isn't also using others, or that if you are married he or she will be true to you. Another outcome of sexual activity that deteriorates the relationship is that usually one partner wants the other one to go farther than he or she wants to go. The first partner then tries to manipulate the other into satisfying his own needs. This takes away the freedom and choice of the partner, and will usually bring on either guilt feelings or resentment. Taking a person beyond the limits where he wishes to go is seduction, whether or not it involves complete sexual activity.

Sex is potentially one of the most rewarding of all life's experiences; at the same time it can be one of the most destructive of all of life's forces. You need to be careful to keep your sexual feelings in check so that they don't begin to dominate your thoughts and time at the expense of other important aspects of your personality. It really helps if you can involve yourself in a variety of activities and a variety of dates so that

UP-DATE

you will have a better chance of developing a mature personality. You might find that developing a mature personality is
more difficult than giving in to your sexual feelings—all the
more reason to learn to control those feelings!

7

What's It Worth?

If two people are going to spend between thirteen and eighteen thousand days and nights of intimacy together, it is extremely important that things that are of value to one partner are also of value to the other. When couples argue over money, time, child-rearing practices, religion, sex, or in-laws, they are really arguing about values. It is the value they place on how the money should be used, or how much time they should spend together, that causes the difficulties.

This partial list of the value systems of one couple shows how destructive conflicting value systems can be to a marriage:

His values	Her values
Self	Self
Sex	Power
Job	Religion
Money	Children
Leisure activities	Family
Peace	Marriage
Religion	Status
Children	Money

As you look at the list, you can see that it is hard for this pair to get along. She controls the marriage because power is important to her, and she uses sex to control him because it is so important to him. She wants him to be involved in church activities, but he would rather spend time on the ski slopes or the tennis courts. He is not home much because he likes his job and money so much. He is upset because she wants to spend so much time with her family and she is upset because he won't spend enough time with the children. Nagging pays off for her because peace is important to him. And so we could go on. When you are dating, you need to become aware of your values and those of your date so you can pick a compatible partner.

Learning to understand your own values and those of your partner is a major part of good dating. To help you, here is a list of values. Put them in order of their importance to you. You might want to make two lists: one in the order that you would like them to be, and another listing them in the order they really assume in your life. None of us live up to our ideal values, so our real values, the ones that reflect our everyday behavior, are the ones that make a difference in marriage.

_____ 1. Self—protecting my own interests
_____ 2. Being right
_____ 3. Feeling needed and wanted
_____ 4. Power—being in charge
_____ 5. Sex
_____ 6. Concern for others
_____ 7. Children
_____ 8. Religion
_____ 9. Individual freedom
_____ 10. Money
_____ 11. Status—popularity
_____ 12. Education
_____ 13. Parental family
_____ 14. Leisure-time activities
_____ 15. Marriage
_____ 16. Peace—lack of conflict
_____ 17. Security
_____ 18. Politics
_____ 19. Job
_____ 20. Appearance
_____ 21. Morals

You need to find basic agreement with your future mate as to the order of the general values. But each separate value can cause a conflict by itself as well, and so merits some individual discussion. A few examples will help you see the kind of discussion you need to have on your dates to insure a better marriage.

1.   Religion: What religion should you follow? How involved should you be in church activities, and what kinds of family practices do you want to participate in?

2.   Education: How important is it? How much should each partner have? How should careers be handled and what should they be?

3.   Money: What kind of life-style do you want to have? Where do you want to live? How do you want to spend your money—on clothes, food, recreation, education, etc.?

4.   Job: Do you want a 9-to-6 husband or someone who is more involved in his work? How much status should his job have? Which is more important, work or play?

5.   Power: Who is going to be the boss, and how should it be decided?

6.   Children: Do you want them? How many? How should they be disciplined? How much time should each parent spend with them?

A good understanding of values—your own as well as your partner's—is essential to a happy marriage.

8

A Look at Your Life-Style

To a young woman, it may seem romantic to marry an Arabian prince, but if she grew up in a typical American home, she might find it difficult to live in a world where she shared her husband with three other wives, she had no say in what happened, her husband owned her like a piece of property, and she couldn't even drive a car.

To either a young man or woman, if you grew up in the Bronx, you might not do well in the mansions of Beverly Hills, or you might find it difficult to live with a person from a small town that had a high school graduating class of seven.

No two people have exactly the same life-style, so one of the most important tasks of your dating days is to come to an understanding of the life-style that best fits you and then to find someone whose life-style is compatible with your own, someone with whom you would enjoy sharing life.

For the most part, your life-style depends on the world you grew up in. Your ethnic background, whether it is Japanese, German, Greek, Indian, or American; your religious background, Hindu, atheist, Catholic, born-again Christian, or Mormon; your economic background, rich, middle-class, or poor; where you live, on a farm, in a ghetto, in a suburb, or in a city—all of these things are a part of the most important ingredient of your life-style, your family. Life-style has to do with such things as your energy level, how your family spends Christmas, how you like to spend your time, and what you eat for breakfast. We are talking about the habits you have developed over a lifetime, the activities you enjoy most, the kinds of people with whom you like to associate, your sleeping habits, and so forth.

Since understanding your own life-style is a major importance, rate yourself on the following questions:

Energy level

1. _____ Do you tend to be active and on the go all the time?
   _X_ Or do you tend to be listless and lackadaisical? *some*
2. _____ Do you tend to be a compulsive worker who has to get things done right away?
   _X_ Or do you tend to procrastinate? *a little*
3. _X_ Do you tend to be organized and methodical?
   _____ Or are you disorganized and cluttered?
4. _sort of_ Do you enjoy working all the time to the exclusion of leisure time?
   _____ Or do you prefer to play and only work to make play possible?
   _X_ Or maybe a combination of both?

not always

Where would you like to live?

_____ on a farm
_____ in a city with population of 5,000-10,000
_X_ 10,000-25,000 population
_____ 100,000-500,000 population
_____ over 500,000 population
_____ inner city
_____ suburb
_____ in an apartment
_____ in your own home
_____ in a condominium

How do you prefer to spend your time?

If you check more than one, put them in order of your preference.

With whom
_1_ Alone
_1_ With girl/boy friend
_____ In small groups
_____ In large groups
_3_ With close friends
_2_ With family

Where
_1_ Indoors
_2_ Outdoors
_1_ Mountains
_3_ City
_____ Beach
_____ Desert
_4_ Home

Doing what
_____ Sleeping
_____ Eating

_____ Watching TV
_X_ Dancing →

43

_____Sports, participating   _X_Going to movies
_____Sports, watching   _X_Engaging in hobbies
_X_Sightseeing   _____Cooking
_X_Reading   _____Sewing
_____Going to school   _X_Shopping
_____Attending parties   _____Visiting
_X_Listening to music (list kind) _____Working
_X_Enjoying fine arts   _____Serving others

Since most of your expectations about life come from your family, you need to ask some special questions about them:

1. How happy is your home life?
2. How does your family resolve conflicts?
3. How do your family members show love to one another?
4. How close is your family?
5. Who is the boss and what does that person do to become boss?
6. How well does your family work together?
7. How does your family have fun together?
8. What does your family do at meal time?
9. What does your family do on holidays?
10. What does your family do on vacation?
11. How organized is your home?
12. How many children are there in your family? How were they disciplined?

The accompanying questionnaire may also be of some value in helping you understand your family and your expectations for marriage roles.

Who does the following activities in your home?

Place an X by the person who usually does the activity.
Place an 0 by the person who occasionally does the activity.
Write the name of the person you would like to see do it, i.e., father, mother, child, etc.

44

Activity	Father	Mother	Child	Other	No one	Who would you like to do it?
1. Who sees that family members get up on time?	X	O				
2. Who makes the beds?			X			
3. Who cleans the bedrooms?			X			
4. Who does the dusting?			X			
5. Who vacuums?		O	X			
6. Who cleans the rest of the house?		X				
7. Who prepares the meals?	O	X	O			
8. Who sets the table?	O	O	X			
9. Who does the dishes?	O	X	O			
10. Who takes out the garbage?	O	O	X			
11. Who takes care of the pets?						
12. Who locks up at night?		O	X			
13. Who mends the family's clothes?						
14. Who fixes broken things, i.e., toys, furniture, appliances?						
15. Who cleans the garage?						
16. Who does the wash?						
17. Who does the ironing?						
18. Who waters the yard?						
19. Who mows the lawn?						
20. Who weeds the yard?						
21. Who takes care of the rest of the yard?						
22. Who picks up and puts away the clothes?						
23. Who punishes the children?						
24. Who teaches the children values?						
25. Who cares for the children when they are sick?						

26. Who sees that the children have fun?						
27. Who sees that the children are clean and dressed?						
28. Who sees that family members get places on time?						
29. Who gets up with the children at night?						
30. Who regulates the children's schedule, i.e., comes in, goes to bed, etc.?						
31. Who teaches the children facts and skills?						
32. Who helps the children with schoolwork?						
33. Who selects the TV programs?						
34. Who makes sure the family has family prayer?						
35. Who makes sure the family has family home evening?						
36. Who plans family home evening?						
37. Who provides the family with money?						
38. Who pays the family bills?						
39. Who shops for groceries?						
40. Who decides on home furnishings?						
41. Who helps the children with money?						
42. Who plans the family investments?						
43. Who plans the family vacation?						
44. Who decides what the family will do on holidays?						
45. Who shops for the family clothes?						
46. Who shops for the family car?						
47. Who repairs the family car?						
48. Who resolves family disputes?						
49. Who returns things to the store?						
50. Who keeps peace with the neighbors?						

Since your life-style has such great effect on your marriage, you need to make sure that you have enough different kinds of dates with a person over a long enough period of time to understand each other's life-style. Be sure your patterns of dealing with life are compatible with your mate's.

9

Relating and Relationships

Developing an intimate relationship with another person is perhaps life's most rewarding experience, as can be attested to by anyone who has an exciting marriage (or wishes he had one). Dating is the place where you learn to relate to others, the time of life when you need most to practice good interpersonal skills.

The following list of attributes that make a relationship great are the ones you should be developing in your own life.

1. Be positive, outgoing, pleasant, and enthusiastic.

2. Share yourself with others. Share your feelings with others, and give them a chance to serve you.

3. Enjoy serving others. Spend time, energy, and resources in their behalf. Do little things for them.

4. Serve in secret. Do things for others without thought of reward or their knowing where the service came from.

5. Be concerned about others' welfare and progression. Help them improve and grow.

6. Enjoy people's company.

7. Respect others as individuals. Allow them to hold opinions and have interests different from your own.

8. Allow others to make mistakes. Do not condemn them for character traits that you do not approve of or agree with.

9. Be understanding and forgiving, patient and kind.

10. Have a wide range of common interests. Enjoy doing a great many things together.

11. Enjoy others' winning. Get as excited about their winning as you do your own. Be willing to lose so they can win.

12. Treat others as equals and expect to be treated the same. Try to create a cooperative atmosphere.

13. Be even-tempered and stable in your moods. Avoid a

lot of ups and downs in your relationships with others.

14. Take the responsibility for the success of your relationships with others, and be committed to their success.

There are three areas that deserve special consideration: concern for the feelings of others, enjoying service, and being responsible for the relationship.

Being Concerned for the Feelings of Others

For most people, dating is a self-motivated experience. People are basically interested only in what dating will do for them. If you go out with someone and all he is able to do is worry about how much fun he is having, you can be sure that person is being immature. Sometimes people with a good "line" will make you think they are really concerned about your feelings when they are not. A young man whose girlfriend became pregnant told her that if she loved him, she would get an abortion. Obviously the young man was not at all concerned about her. He was only concerned about his own reputation. A word of caution: concern for the feelings of others or the desire to be liked by others should never cause you to violate those principles that are sacred to you.

When looking for "the one and only," one way you can judge a person's concern for the feelings of others is to see how he or she treats family members. If people show little concern for their parents or other family members, the chances are pretty good that they will treat their marriage partners the same way.

Serving Others

Since marriage and family living involve learning to live with others, finding happiness in serving others is an essential part of good dating. Look for the person who performs little unexpected services or does things without being asked. I remember a beautiful young girl who was a straight-A student, president of her high school student body, and an accomplished musician. At socials when someone had to stay to clean up, she was always willing to volunteer. When something needed to be done at home, she willingly did it. I once heard her mother say that she often came home to a clean house; the work, of course, was done by the daughter. I'm sure you can guess what kind of wife and mother she became.

An important trait for those who enjoy serving others is not to be afraid of work. In fact, most people who find joy in service also find happiness in work.

Being Responsible for Your Actions

One of the side effects of Freudian philosophy is the tendency to blame someone else—mother, father, environment—for one's own problems. Add to that the "I have a right to do my own thing" concept, along with the current notion of immediate gratification of needs, and you have created a monster. People want *what* they want *when* they want it without paying the price. If you want to be a good date or a good marriage partner, you must learn what the costs are and be willing to pay the price.

To be a good date, you must take the responsibility of seeing that your date has a good time. This may mean that you have to sacrifice your own needs and desires or keep them in check for later gratification. A responsible person learns to do this willingly.

A responsible person should avoid being overly defensive—irresponsible people have a tendency to make excuses or to justify themselves. A responsible person also does not procrastinate. He does what has to be done when it needs to be done. He makes good use of his time. He doesn't shrink from responsibility. He also completes tasks rather than leaves them unfinished.

10
Developing Your Social Skills

Knowing how to treat another person is vital to successful dating. Like anything else you do in life, the more you practice social skills, the better you become at them. The more you use good skills, the more confident you become and the more dates you get. Let's start at the beginning.

Boys, how do you ask a girl for a date? Two things should be remembered. First, girls don't like to play games when boys call them, particularly on the first date. Don't telephone her and play the "guess who" game for twenty minutes. If she is smart, she will turn you down right away. The second no-no is to ask her, "What are you doing Saturday night?" With that, she will probably be busy. Besides, there may be certain kinds of dates she may not be able to go on or may not want to go on. By asking her directly, you can avoid any embarrassment to you both. The rule, then, is to tell her who you are when you call, when you would like the date, and what you would like to do. Generally speaking, short conversations are better when you are first getting to know each other. You may lose points with long telephone conversations.

Girls, if you want to go with him, accept his invitation and find out when he will pick you up and what you should wear. If you don't want to go with him, then be honest and let him know. Ninety-eight percent of the hundreds of college-age men I have asked prefer a girl to be direct and turn them down rather than make up excuses or go when they do not want to. You might try an approach like this: "Thanks for asking me; I really appreciate your friendship, but I don't think we would enjoy going together." Most boys have been turned down before, so they know what it is like and they will live through it. Cheap excuses will only tell him something about your social ineptness.

If you really want to go with him, but he asks you for a time when you cannot go, you can really boost his ego by saying, "I'm sorry, I'll be busy that day, but I really would like to go with you some other time." You might even suggest an alternative, such as, "We're going bike riding Saturday morning. Would you like to come with us?" You already know he cares about you because he asked you in the first place, so it isn't too bold to invite him in this manner.

It is true that you should take some risks and go out with some of those boys you don't think will be good dates, because often they turn out to be better than you think. I know many people who, before their first date, really didn't want to go out with the person they eventually married. You ought to take some risks, but if you really don't want to go out with someone, be honest.

Boys, don't push your luck or shatter your ego. Ask her for one, maybe two, separate dates at the same time. If she turns you down, say okay and wait for a week or so before asking her again. If she turns you down again, you should probably get the message.

The big night comes. The first rule is to be on time. If you are going to be late, you owe each other the courtesy of calling and letting your date know. Girls, if it is a first date, the person who greets him at the door should not be mom or dad or little sister. It should be you. It really is inconsiderate to make a boy come in and spend fifteen minutes trying to make conversation with your father, whom he has never met before, while you finish getting ready. You should meet him at the door and then bring him in to introduce him to your family. Be sure that the first visit is brief.

Give the boy an opportunity to be a gentleman. Hand him your coat so that he can help you on with it. Pause at the door; do not go bolting out into the night without him. Take his arm and he will think you are a real lady.

When you get to the car, if he forgets to open the door for you, just hold onto his arm and when he starts walking around to his side say, "Oh, I didn't know you intended for me to drive." Or just stand on the curb and watch him drive off into the sunset; when he notices you are not there, he will probably get the idea.

When you get into the car, you don't have to slide over and sit on his lap; neither do you need to cling to the door as if you were ready to jump out at the next stop sign. Perhaps somewhere in between would be appropriate—close enough to make him feel wanted, but not so close as to suggest that he has privileges that he really does not have.

Girls, one of the best things you can do when you are out with a boy is to treat him like a king. Now, that doesn't mean that you have to do anything improper, but it does mean that you are attentive and concerned about him. You hold his arm, and you let him know that you are glad to be with him. The girl who gets the repeat dates is the one who makes the boy's ego feel six stories high—that is a lot more important than kisses or anything else. Treat him with interest, use eye contact, introduce him to people you know, don't flirt with other boys, don't talk about other dates, and don't pretend you are with someone else.

Find something you like about your date and let him or her know it. Compliment each other on things you sincerely feel are good. It is important that you learn to share dreams and feelings. Dating provides a great opportunity to learn to share.

A simple refresher of some good etiquette rules: If there is an usher or waiter to seat you, the girl goes first. If not, the boy leads. If you go to eat before or after a function, the boy should always have enough cash with him to buy two orders of the most expensive item on the menu, whether it is a "Big Mac" or a steak. Don't be in the position of the girl ordering prime rib and you having to order a pine float. (For those who don't know, a pine float is a toothpick floating on water.)

Boys, when you make the date, be sure you let the girl know if dinner is intended. It is embarrassing for a girl who has just eaten a big dinner to have to fake enjoying more food soon afterward.

Girls, if you order something, order what you can eat and eat it. Don't just order any old thing and then leave it. Even if it is just a diet salad, *relish it.*

Boys, let the girl know what you are going to order so she has some idea of what is appropriate. She will feel more at ease and know what she is expected to do.

Now the difficult part. You are taking her home. The girl does not owe the boy anything for the date except her attention and kind treatment. You do not owe each other anything physical. You should never stay in the car very long, especially on the first few dates. Don't make your date uncomfortable by keeping him or her longer than you should.

Girls, when he takes you to the front door, if he tries to move in, just take hold of both hands and stiffen your arms—the old arm's-length adage in practice. If all else fails, you can always lean on the doorbell and have the lights flash on, or poke him in the eye with a sharp stick, but it seems to me that something a little more subtle would produce better results.

Here again, sincerely feeding his ego is better than physical involvement. Tell him that you had a great time and really enjoyed his company. Let him know you would like to go with him again. If he gets the feeling that you care about him and that you are interested in him, you will accomplish more in the long run than if you give in physically.

Remember, any time you do anything physical with one another, it should always be an expression of the relationship and not a self-indulgent experience. Some people kiss or neck merely to gratify their selfish desires. If you really care about someone and want to express it in a physical way, meaning "I think you are extra special," then it is unlikely that you would ever do it inappropriately. You would be more concerned with the feelings and standards of the other person and more concerned with the relationship than with self-gratification.

Overcoming Distasteful Habits and Mannerisms

Some may have a difficult time dating the people who might make the best partners for them because they have distasteful habits and mannerisms, and other people do not want to be around them.

The following is a list of habits and mannerisms that students at the Brigham Young University found distasteful in a date. You might look and see how many of them you might have that need to be changed. They are divided into four categories.

UP-DATE
1. Physical Habits
Biting fingernails
Having unclean and uneven fingernails
Dressing sloppily
Picking nose
Not looking date in the eyes while talking
X Chewing gum
Spitting
Chewing with mouth open
Picking pimples
Having bad breath
Burping
Coughing without covering mouth
Having sloppy makeup
Putting makeup on in public
Wearing sagging nylons
Having greasy hair
Cracking knuckles
Not brushing teeth
X Wearing too much cologne or aftershave
Picking food out of teeth
Wearing inappropriate clothing
Picking fingernail polish off

2. Manners
Being impolite
Drinking from bowl
Slouching at the table
Always fixing hair or touching up
X Not eating all the food ordered
Sticking gum on plate
Using fingers while eating
Eating too fast
Walking in front of date
Swearing, drinking, smoking
Using poor English
Honking for date
Not knowing the proper way to eat

54

3. Interpersonal Habits

Being late
Flirting with others
Having no opinion of own
Acting superior to date
Driving recklessly
Showing off
Not being considerate of others
Not allowing him to be a gentleman
Not caring about anything
Thinking date owes him a kiss
Not coming to the door to get date
Not knowing when to leave
Girls opening doors for selves
Not introducing date to friends
Putting self down
Complaining or apologizing for dress
Acting unreal
Acting afraid
Getting offended easily
Tickling
Being too aggressive
Not having decided what to do
Being impatient while driving
Leaving date alone at party
Always needing to be center of attention
Giving waitress a bad time
Changing date after picking girl up
Coming too early
Correcting date's driving
Comparing date to others
Making fun of sentimental things
Making a scene in public
Not calling when going to be late
Having mind on other things
Acting unfeminine
Walking too fast for date
Watching other girls or guys
Parking
Poking date

4. Conversation Habits

Talking about other dates
Gossiping
Bringing up things that are inappropriate
Telling crude or dumb jokes
Doing all the talking
Putting date down
Being too loud
Being too agreeable
Refusing to give opinion
X Giggling
X Always talking about the good old days
Telling friends what date talked about
Laughing too much
Interrupting
X Being opinionated
Nagging
Insulting
Talking to others on phone while date is there
Always being critical
Keeping silent
Talking only about sports or other pet subjects
Repeating the same story or question

X Teasing

11
Sharing a Secret

One of the most important aspects of any relationship —on a date, at home, at school, at work—is the ability to communicate effectively. There are many definitions of communication, but the one that seems to describe best what is necessary for good dating and marriage is given by John Powell: "Our word, *communication*, refers to a process by which someone or something is made common, that is, it is shared. If you tell me a secret, then you and I possess the knowledge of your secret in common, and you have communicated it to me." (*Why Am I Afraid to Tell You Who I Am* [Argus Communications, 1969], p. 7.) The key to this definition is *sharing*. Communication does not take place unless we come to understand the world as the other person sees it.

Many messages are sent and received that are not intended and usually not accurately perceived. This, by our definition, does not count as communication. To count as communication, the message sent, verbally or nonverbally, must be exactly the same one that is received.

There are two phases to good communication: understanding and resolution. Most problems are made worse by skipping the understanding phase, whereas many problems are resolved when understanding takes place. To become good at communicating, you need to practice stopping at understanding without trying to resolve the problem. The next time you have a problem with someone, try to thoroughly understand each other. When you feel understanding is complete, stop for a drink of water before trying to solve the problem.

The Understanding Phase
Before you can understand or be understood by another

person, you must have some understanding of yourself. Good communication cannot take place unless you are honest with yourself about your own feelings. Perhaps when you have feelings that you think other people will not approve of, you tend to try to hide them. When you have practiced this long enough, you are not sure how you really do feel. Remember when you were a child and you said to your mother, "I hate you," and your father said, "You'd better not hate your mother or I'll clobber you." Suddenly you were not supposed to feel what you really felt, and soon you didn't know how you felt. To communicate successfully, you must be willing to look at yourself and to recognize how you really feel. If you have feelings that you think are inappropriate, you might want to change them, but never try to ignore them.

Everyone has a mind-set or a way of looking at the world that comes from family and culture. Each family and culture has its own mind-set. You know the person who always says, "Don't confuse me with the facts; my mind is made up." We may not be as bad as that, but all of us have mind-sets that make it hard to see another person's point of view. The more rigid one's point of view (mind-set), the less able he is to communicate. Since a person generally feels that his interpretation about any issue is correct, he often can't hear what another person is trying to communicate. We all tend to judge, to evaluate, to approve of, or to disapprove of other people and their communications. Our mind-sets decide for us what those judgments will be.

We also send every message through an "emotional filter." Your perception of a message is always affected if you are angry, hurt, happy, or sad. So understanding your own emotional state is important to good communication.

The second essential condition to understanding is an awareness of your own motives. Often, communication is designed to be one-way. People are not concerned with the feelings of others, only that their own needs are met. To this end their communication is often used to manipulate the other person into meeting their needs or into being the person they want him or her to be. To accomplish this, people put on facades, deceive, or reveal only parts of themselves.

Most people are usually so busy trying to convert others or

defending their own position that they can't hear what is being said. If I assume that I am always right and that anyone who disagrees with me is wrong, then my task is to point out to him the error of his position and the validity of my own.

If another person disagrees or points out my weaknesses or differences, I feel that I am being attacked. The only thing I can do, therefore, is quit listening and build my case against my adversary. Often in a situation like this, people are so afraid of being rejected that they let others see only what they think they will approve of.

The most important motive for successful communication is the desire on the part of each person to understand the other and be understood by him no matter how painful that might be. This requires a willingness to be honest and to disclose who you are. The fewer secrets you have, especially in marriage, the better the communication.

One of the essential ingredients in disclosure is liking one's self. If you are doing things that are contrary to your value system or that might make the people you are talking to reject you, you will try to hide those things. You need to let others see who you really are so that you can say, "What you see is what you get." Your object should be to help the other person understand your feelings, values, perceptions, wants, and needs—in other words, the real you.

Many people think they can communicate if they are honest with one another. While openness and honesty are important to effective communication, you can be honest without understanding and still not be communicating. We often hear people say that they can communicate because they can say how they really feel. Disclosure is important to good communication, but just because you disclose something, it does not necessarily follow that you are being understood by the other person.

The nature of a relationship has a great deal to do with the quality of the communication. Where the relationship is strained, and if those involved are angry, hurt, or tired, communication tends to break down. If you are afraid that your communication will injure your relationship with the other person, you either avoid the communication or you give a censored version of how you really feel. Sometimes you are fearful that the other person won't understand you or that you will be rejected. If I go to lunch with the boys at the office, and if I think that my wife will chew me out for going, I probably won't tell her about it. Often people don't share their feelings because of their own self-image. If you want to be seen in a certain way, and how you feel is not consistent with that image, you might try to hide your feelings.

Three important attributes of a good relationship are:

Mutual trust—if you feel you can trust someone with your feelings and know they will try to understand you, you are more willing to be yourself.

Mutual respect—if you respect someone and his or her judgment, you are more willing to share.

Mutual esteem—you also communicate more effectively with those you think highly of or care a great deal about.

In trying to develop and improve your relationship with another person, you need to decide what is important and worth pursuing, and what is of little value and unnecessary. There are many issues that might make life more comfortable, but are not very relevant to the whole of life. Expanding your level of tolerance and acceptance of the other person helps you grow and improves your "dateability."

Sending to Be Understood

To be a successful sender you must create an atmosphere in which both you and the other person feel free to be your real selves. Your feeling should be, "I want you to understand who I really am; and I am willing to take the risk of rejection and misunderstanding to have you know me so that our relationship can grow." To do this, you need to talk in such a way that the other person doesn't feel defensive, that he is to blame for your feelings, that you are trying to change him, that you are trying to make him over, put him down, or get even with him. To create this atmosphere you must be willing to:

1. *Own your own feelings.* Some years ago a father killed his son. When asked why he did it, he said, "My wife drove me to it." A young man whose marriage is falling apart because of his drinking says that if his wife were different, then he wouldn't be depressed, he wouldn't drink, and their marriage

would be perfect. Probably all of us could say that if the world were exactly what we wanted it to be, we would always be happy and never get angry, hurt, or depressed.

However, if you want to develop a meaningful relationship with another person, you must be willing to accept the responsibility for your own emotions. In the long run you are responsible in any case. No one is holding a gun at your head forcing you to feel depressed, hurt, angry, happy, or excited. These are feelings you choose to have in each particular situation. If free agency is a true principle, then no one but you causes your feelings. It may be true that you have no control of the world around you, but you are in charge of your emotional response to it.

To communicate well, you must say, "Since these are my emotions, I want to tell you about them in such a way that you won't feel responsible for them." It's helpful to use statements like:

"I may be wrong, but this is how I feel."

"It's not your fault, but when you _____, I feel _____."

"I feel _____ when _____ happens." Be specific about your feelings.

2. *Be tentative.* Most of us assume that on every issue from politics to religion our position is the correct one. Anyone who doesn't agree with us probably doesn't see the world clearly, but with our help, he will come to know the truth. We can always rationalize our point of view.

No matter how bright you are, you can't know all there is to know about every subject. Alexander Magoun once said, "You need to carefully distinguish between your own interpretation of a situation and the actual situation. Each of us must realize and accept our lack of complete knowledge in every situation. Any good mind knows that ideas are relative and that only partial truth is possible for anyone."

A friend and I were once eyewitnesses to an automobile accident. We knew it was going to happen, but despite the advance warning we almost accused the wrong person. Like my perception of the accident, your perceptions may not be accurate. In your quest to create an atmosphere of understanding, you must acknowledge that there may be an outside chance

—no matter how slim—that your position may be wrong.

To do this, use statements like:

"I may be wrong, but . . ."

"It's probably my fault, but . . ."

"I may not understand correctly, but . . ."

"This is how I feel about . . ."

"It seems to me . . ."

"In my opinion . . ."

"I believe . . ."

"It appears to me . . ."

3. *Be specific.* People often talk to each other in such general terms that messages are usually not understood. You need to take the time to give specific data and specific examples to make your point. Describe what you actually see and feel, not your interpretation of the situation. Make sure as you give examples that you don't get sidetracked by the example; stick to the issues.

4. *Some helpful hints.* Be tactful, considerate, and courteous. There is a difference between expressing feelings and venting emotions. Honesty without kindness is cruelty.

Listen to Understand

King Benjamin suggests that there are three important ingredients in effective listening. He said, "Open your ears that ye may hear, and your hearts that ye may understand, and your minds that the mysteries of God may be unfolded to your view." (Mosiah 2:9.) Most people listen with their ears but fail to make their hearts and minds available. They are usually so busy thinking of what they are going to say that they don't hear the full message. If your desire is to understand the other person's world more clearly, you must be willing to make available not only your ears, but your heart and mind also.

Accept the other person's right to feel, think, perceive, and act differently than you expect or want him to. Everyone has the right to be an individual and to express himself as he desires. No matter how much alike you are, there will be some differences.

Assume that the other person has a good reason for acting and feeling the way he does. Every emotion makes sense to that person at the time he is feeling it. The task of the listener is to see why the other person feels the way he does. Pay attention to his nonverbal as well as his verbal messages.

Never try to read someone's mind. Check out your assumptions about his feelings. Ask questions that reflect your caring and desire to understand. Don't just parrot back what you hear, but try to rephrase it in terms of the person's underlying motives, values, and assumptions.

Some don'ts:

1. Don't interrupt. You will get your chance.
2. Don't lose your "cool."
3. Don't intellectualize.
4. Don't interrogate.
5. Don't get defensive or don't worry about blame.

The Resolution Phase—Learning to Negotiate

When we think of negotiation, we usually think of countries working to resolve international crises or a labor union trying to reach a contract agreement with management. In either case, each side decides what it is willing to give up in order that both parties might reach an agreement. Dr. Tessa Albert-Warschaw calls this process "trade-offs." If you are going to negotiate successfully you must decide what you are willing to sacrifice (trade) to obtain the rewards that you feel are important. Dr. Albert-Warschaw states, "A negotiator must realize that his or her behavior won't cause the other person to change miraculously. The real power in negotiation is that *you* change. As you change, others around you will have to change because you are different. You are the one who has to do it."

In every worthwhile endeavor there are prices to be paid and few bargains. The intelligent person learns what his goals cost and pays the price with a willing heart. To negotiate successfully you must clarify and prioritize your values and goals. You need to decide what lower-priority goals you are willing to sacrifice in order to achieve your higher-priority goals. Many people fail to negotiate because they don't want to give up any of their goals or make any changes. They want the other person to make all the changes. This of course creates an impasse that leads to wars between nations and in marriages.

It might be well to keep in mind the origin of the word *sacrifice*. It comes from two Greek words, *sacra* and *ficio*, meaning to make holy or to give up something of value for the sake of something or someone more valuable.

Practice the "win-win" principle where both people want to be sure that both end up as winners. If your desire is to win every time you negotiate, you may win all the battles and still lose the war. If you do win every time there is a disagreement, you will probably begin to destroy the relationship. In many relationships, such as selling, you negotiate with another person only once, so winning at his expense isn't quite as disastrous. But when you have to live and negotiate with the same person day in and day out, you both need to feel like winners. Often people act as if each negotiation were the one and only one—winning becomes everything. Remember that if you let the other person win this time, it might bring you closer together and you may win the next time. It is important that you always keep the other person and his feelings in mind when you make your point.

To be a successful negotiator in dating, you need to become aware of both your own and the other person's response patterns:

1. How do you present your case? By acting as an expert witness, an interrogator, a forceful authority, a humble servant, a martyr, a "dumb blonde" seeking help, someone seeking information, or someone seeking understanding?

2. How do you solve problems? When there is a disagreement, how do you respond? Compromise? Give in? Withdraw? Become hostile? Put the other person down? Postpone the decision? Agree to disagree?

3. How do you respond when you are losing or are victimized? When you are winning? Who has the power and how is it gained?

Don't bring up past injuries when trying to resolve today's problems. In marriage and dating, grudges and past injuries are of little constructive value. If the same issues are brought up repeatedly, then clearly your techniques are not working and you need some improvement. If the same issues are brought up more than three or four times, then apparently neither of you is willing to change and all you are trying to do is convert each other. At that point you should both sit down and look at your goals again.

In marriage and in other long-term relationships it is helpful to identify areas of expertise for each person. Once this is determined, it is smart to decide on spheres of authority. Decide which problems fit into each person's sphere of authority; in those areas that person has the final say. Naturally it is extremely helpful to have those affected by the decision help in the decision-making process.

Design a strategy. Clarify the options, identify as many solutions as you can, and talk about the pros and cons of each. You may want to redefine the problem. Say it in a different way or look at it from a different angle. Don't try to resolve the issue until both of you have exhausted all your alternatives. Planning ahead helps you keep your cool.

Execute your plan with self-confidence and bold action. Don't be intimidated, and don't become defensive or put the other person on the defensive. Take the risk necessary to succeed.

When things get really tense, diversion is suggested. A good sense of humor is really helpful; don't take yourself too seriously. Expressions of respect, affection, and concern will relieve a lot of tension. Switching roles and changing your routine can usually provide some helpful additional insights.

It is very helpful to keep a record of what is happening, what works, and what doesn't work. Be specific about your own reactions and those of the other person. A diary or journal will help both of you be more successful the next time you negotiate.

12

This Thing Called Love

In our society the feeling we call "love" plays such an important part in deciding who we date and who we marry that we need to give it special consideration. Love is a very difficult word to define.

Let us ask again about the differences in the love I have for my wife and the love I have for ice cream, sports cars, football, my Boy Scout troop, or my dog. The differences may not be so much in the *definition* of the word love as in the *nature of the relationship.* When I say I love ice cream what I mean is that I want the ice cream to cease to exist as ice cream and begin to exist as a part of me. That is exploitation. When I say I love football, I mean I get a thrill out of playing or watching football, which is self-gratification. When I say I love my Boy Scout troop, I might mean that they build my ego or that I find satisfaction in service. Love for my dog might mean I enjoy his loyalty or the fact that he can't talk back. The love I have for my wife might involve exploitation, possession, self-gratification, ego fulfillment, service, loyalty, and many other things.

Maybe the best definition of love is that it is an emotional affinity toward someone or something. If we use this definition, then any difference isn't in the definition but in the nature of the relationship and the intensity of the emotion. The intensity of my feelings for my wife, my children, and my mother is about the same, but the nature of the relationship with each is different. When we compare my love for football with my love for my wife, not only is the relationship different but the intensity of it is as well. (On some Monday nights she thinks I love football more, but I certainly don't interact the same with my wife as I do with football.)

Of the intensity of love, O. Ohmann states, "The intensity of a love affair is no guarantee of its permanence. On the contrary, an intensely felt love may indicate neurotic anxiety, while a less emotional affair may mean greater maturity and self-sufficiency." (As quoted in *You and Marriage*, Peter M. Jordan, ed. [New York: Wiley Publishers, 1942], p. 28.)

If your dating is to help you develop the kind of love that will create a good marriage, there are some important aspects of the relationship you need to consider.

1. What is it about the other person that turns you on emotionally? Is it her good looks, her sparkling personality, or her father's money? You need to know if what attracts you will last a lifetime or not.

2. What is it in you that is being turned on? Is it your need for security, reassurance, sense of belonging, importance, romance? Sometimes we love people because they help us solve some special problems or escape from a family or job situation, economic insecurity, social or religious rejection. You need to know what is going on inside yourself.

Love is not love unless it is expressed in action. Everyone has an idea of how people should act when they are in love. Often the way one partner expects love to be shown and the way the other person would like it to be shown are so far apart that it is destructive to the relationship.

A young man said to his wife, "You don't love me." Her response was, "How do you know?" He: "Our sex life has been zero lately." She: "That really makes me mad. I do too love you. Don't you remember when you were sick last week and I fixed your favorite food? What do you think I was trying to tell you?" For the young man love was sex, and for his wife love was service. Both of their attempts at showing love were unrecognized.

You need to begin to resolve this serious problem while dating. You need to learn to recognize how you want love to be expressed and how your date likes it expressed. There are really four questions that deal with expectations for love that you need to have answered.

1. How I feel I should act if I love someone.
2. How I feel she/he should act if she/he loves me.
3. How she/he feels I should show my love for her/him.
4. How she/he feels she/he should show her/his love for me.

UP-DATE

To help you see the importance of this problem, ask your parents or some other married couple to answer the following questions:

1. How does Dad/Mom show you he/she loves you?
2. How do you show Dad/Mom that you love him/her?
3. How would Dad/Mom like you to show him/her your love?
4. How would you like Dad/Mom to show you he/she loves you?

If you ask both parents and get conflicting answers, you will see how vital it is that this problem of the expression of love be resolved during your dating days.

The love we have been talking about so far has been concerned with your feelings as a result of your involvement with another person. There is another way of looking at love that is important to dating. This kind of love is a personality trait, exemplified by people like Albert Schweitzer and Mahatma Ghandi who were willing to make tremendous personal sacrifices for their people. Perhaps the best example of this kind of love was shown by Jesus Christ, who willingly gave his life for his friends.

This kind of love has nothing to do with the way others treat you but rather with how you treat others. The Bible describes this loving kind of person as one who finds happiness in service to others; who is patient and kind; never jealous or boastful, conceited, proud, arrogant, or rude; who does not hold grudges or keep track of wrongs done by others; who is not irritable or touchy; who never rejoices in injustice but rejoices in the truth. This kind of love is true at all costs, believes the best of people, and endures the hardship caused by that love.

If I were dating, this is the kind of love I would want to develop in myself and would look for in the person I wanted to marry. These people are obviously the best dates and the best mates.

13

Your Dateability Rating

Rate yourself as a date by taking the quiz that follows. If you score very low, the first thing you have to do is look at those areas where your score was low on the test and see what you can do to improve. It might mean that you have to go on a weight-control program, have someone teach you how to put on makeup, or get involved in some new activities. Mostly, you might need to work on your personality. If you scored high on the test and still are not getting dates, one of two things must be wrong: either you were not honest or you are not making yourself available.

Everything starts with the first impression, so make it a good one. You can never get to first base if you never get up to bat. People will judge you by the way you look and what they think your personality is like. Your grooming is important—and since not all people agree on what a well-dressed person looks like, you need to dress to impress the group of friends you would like to be noticed by. How you fix your hair and makeup will make a difference, and in our society, weight plays a large part in your chance to get a date. But as stated earlier, personality has more to do with your chances of getting a date than your looks do. If you appear cheerful and outgoing, then you will be seen as a fun date.

Once you get that first date, making sure you get asked out again requires a different set of skills. It is important that you appear to be self-confident. (See chapter 5.) If you appear poised and in control and as if you are having fun, you are way ahead on points.

Making your dates feel that you are interested in them and making them feel important are the keys to good dating. Richard H. Klemer has said, "Fancy clothes, expensive automobiles, and aftershave lotion are relatively impotent when compared to the addicting power of being able to understand, reassure, and respond to another person." (*Marriage and Family Relationships* [New York: Harper and Row, 1970], p. 77.)

Boys, all you need to do is be where the girls are that you want to date and let your sparkling personality come through. Then all you need is the courage to ask her. If you are getting turned down a lot, you may not be as dateable as you thought you were, or you may be asking girls that are out of your league.

Girls have a somewhat different problem. Although it is becoming more acceptable for girls to ask boys for dates, most girls feel it is still the boy's role to do the asking. If you want to ask a boy out, however, the same rules apply to girls as to boys. It might be helpful in developing social skills if you take advantage of the opportunity to ask a boy for a date.

You probably know some girls who would flunk the test yet still seem to get all the dates they want, but that is probably because they are willing to let the boys treat them like objects and are willing to do whatever the boys want. This may work during the few years of dating, but it does little to make a great marriage partner.

National statistics indicate that there are one hundred girls in the usual marriage-age range for every ninety-five boys, so girls, you can't stay at home and wait for him to break your door down; there are too many others he can chase. The most important thing you can do is let him know you exist. Try the following:

1. Take a class that has mostly boys in it, such as auto mechanics, woodworking, chemistry, or maybe even boys' choir.

2. Study on the steps of the engineering building or the boys' gym.

3. In the crowded lunchroom sit next to some cute guys and strike up a conversation.

4. Ask a boy if the seat next to him in the library or at church is taken.

5. Ask someone to help you with your homework, in his favorite subject.

6. Have someone help you fix your car.

7. Have him teach you to play tennis.

8. Ask him some big religious or philosophical questions.

9. Work on a committee with him. Make sure the chairperson asks the one you want.

10. Be involved in group activities.

11. Get the locker next to him.

12. If everything else fails, trip him in the hall.

Here is a quick personality checklist of those who seem to get the most dates:

_X_ 1. Self-confident
_X_ 2. Poised
_X_ 3. Outgoing
_X_ 4. Cheerful
_X_ 5. Able to enjoy life
_X_ 6. Even-tempered
_X_ 7. Dependable
_X_ 8. Concerned for others' feelings
___ 9. Generous
_X_ 10. Intelligent (has varied interests) music

If you are doing all of the things mentioned in this section, you should be getting all the dates you want.

Your Rating as a Date

This is not a test to determine your worth as a person, only your dateability. Many of the most successful adults were not the most dateable teenagers.

We have found that it is difficult to rate yourself as a date because scores seem to be more reflective of your self-image than your dateability. So it would be helpful if you had two or three friends (one of the opposite sex, if possible) and maybe your parents rate you.

Determine the answer that is most indicative of who you are, and write the number of points in the space provided at the right of the question. Remember, this test is no more accurate than you are honest.

I. Dating History

1. Frequency: _____
   a. never   -10
   b. two or three times a year   -5

c.	once a month	-1
d.	two or three times a month	0
e.	once a week or more often	+3

2. Satisfaction with the number of dates: _____
   a. I have too few dates — (-5)
   b. I have too many dates — -3
   c. I have as many dates as I want — +3
3. Satisfaction with the people I date: _____
   a. I very seldom get asked by those I
      would like to date — -5
   b. I usually go out with people I enjoy — +1
   c. I always go out with people I enjoy — (+3)

II. *Physical Aspects*

1. Do your friends consider you: _____
   a. very good-looking — +5
   b. good-looking — (+3)
   c. of average looks — 0
   d. plain — -3
   e. homely — -5
2. Weight _____
   a. if you are within + or - 5 lbs. of
      what you should weigh — (+5)
   b. for each additional 5 lbs. over
      what you should weigh — -3
3. Height _____
   a. girls between 5'3" and 5'8" — +3
   b. boys between 5'8" and 6'3" — +3
   c. for each inch above or below the   -2
      given range — -1
4. Shape _____
   a. good — (+3)
   b. fair — +1
   c. poor — -1
   d. bad — -3

5. Add one point for each one of the following features
that is above average for you and subtract one point for each

that is below average for you; subtract two points if the feature is really bad. If features are average score no points.

a.	hair	+ 1
b.	nose	+ 1
c.	mouth (teeth)	+ 1
d.	hands	+ 1
e.	complexion	+ 1
f.	makeup (for girls)	
g.	muscles (for boys)	+ 1

6. If you have a physical handicap, subtract from 5 to 25 points depending on how that would affect your chances of getting a date. _____

7. Dress—are your clothes:

a.	considered "in" by your friends	+1	
b.	conservative	+1	
c.	appropriate for the occasion	+1	X
d.	varied and attractive	+1	X
e.	well fitting	+1	
f.	extreme in style	-1	
g.	sloppy	-1	
h.	in poor taste	-1	

III. Personality

1. Check each of the following categories that describes you, and add one point for each check.

a.	feminine (for girls)	
b.	masculine (for boys)	X
c.	outgoing	X
d.	well-informed	X
e.	good conversationalist	X
f.	fun-loving	X
g.	sense of humor	X
h.	involved in extracurricular activities	X
i.	willing to try new activities	X
j.	cheerful	X
k.	genuine	X

l. considerate ✗
m. willing to share ✗
n. sentimental ✗
o. talented ✗
p. hard-working ✗
q. intelligent ✗
r. well-mannered ✗
s. religious ✗
t. courteous ✗
u. gentle ✗
v. positive ✗
w. polite ✗
x. neat ✗
y. enthusiastic ✗
z. dependable ✗
aa. confident ✗
bb. affectionate ✗
cc. self-confident ✗
dd. has a variety of interests ✗
ee. enjoys being with people ✗
ff. is concerned for the feelings of others ✗
gg. meets others' needs ✗

2. Check each of the following categories that describes you, and subtract one point for each check.

a. immature for age ___
b. silly ___
c. negative ___
d. too quiet ___
e. uncreative ___
f. pessimistic ___
g. too aggressive ___
h. puts other people down ___
i. gossips ___
j. moody ___
k. lazy ___
l. poor self-image ___
m. too passive ___

n. insults others ___
o. tight with money ___
p. has to be center of attention ___
q. vulgar ___
r. rude ___
s. loud *sometimes* (*not usually*) ___
t. procrastinates ___
u. "plays games" on dates ___
v. not affectionate ___
w. quick-tempered ___

3. If you tend to be selfish, subtract from
5 to 10 points depending on how selfish you are. ___

4. If you have a good self-image and show self-
confidence, give yourself an additional 3 to 8
points. *+7*

5. If you spend a lot of time daydreaming or
reading romantic novels or pornography,
subtract 3 to 8 points. ___

6. If you tend to be rigid and don't see other
points of view, subtract from 3 to 8 points. ___

7. If you have a serious emotional problem,
subtract from 5 to 15 points, depending on how
adversely it affects your dating. ___

IV. Relating to Others
1. Subtract one point for each distasteful habit
and mannerism you have. ___
2. Give yourself one point for each of the following:
a. I get along well with different types of people. *X*
b. I have friends that I have had for a long time. *X*
c. I like to be around people. *X*
d. I do not get angry when people disagree
    with me. *depends who it is (not usually)* *X*
e. I enjoy doing things for others. *X*
f. I am concerned about the feelings of others. *X*
g. I like to belong to groups. *X*

75

UP-DATE
h. I have a number of close friends.   X
i. I enjoy making new friends.   X
j. I like to share my positive feelings about others   X
   with them.
k. I like to do things for other people.   X

3. Subtract one point for each of the following:
   a. I am not content if I don't get my way.   —
   b. I put myself first.
   c. I can hold a grudge.   — \   X
   d. I try to hide my weaknesses.   —
   e. My feelings are easily hurt.   —
   f. I pass on gossip.
   g. I need to be the center of attention.
   h. I enjoy being alone more than with other
      people.   —
   i. I dwell on other people's weaknesses.   —
   j. I feel really insecure.   —
   k. Other people do not enjoy working with me.   —

Add up your score. If your score is above 60, you should be dating all you want. If your score is from 40 to 59, you are still in the ball park. If you score from 20 to 39, you are only a fair date. From 0 to 19 you had better get to work on a self-improvement program. Below 0 means you have a long way to go. If you score very high and are not dating much, you are deceiving yourself.

PART 2

DATES THAT RATE

Part II

Dates that Rate

To help you be more successful, we are including a number of things you might want to try on your dates. The better you get to know your partner, the better your chances of a good marriage.

This list is not all-inclusive; every local area has some exciting things to do. In Seattle you can go to the Seattle Center, boat on Lake Washington, or take the ferry to Victoria. In Los Angeles you can go to Disneyland, to Universal City for the taping of a TV show, or spend a day at the beach. In Salt Lake City you can go to Trolley Square or the Park City Alpine Slide or to the mountains for a day of skiing. Be sure to take advantage of activities going on in your community. Your local newspaper will always have a list of events going on in your town. Also read the local college newspaper; there are always things going on around a college or university.

You might want to mix and match the following ideas and see what exciting dates you can come up with on your own.

Remember that who you are with has far more to do with the success of your date than what you do; therefore, none of these things will be of help to you if you do not choose the right person to do them with.

A word of caution—please be sure that when any date involves the use of someone else's property (such as using a school parking lot for a dance or dinner), you have permission from the authority in charge of that property. Abide by all local laws and ordinances (such as in planning dates for hunting or fishing), and use discretion in planning dates that might infringe on the rights or privacy of others. Have fun—but keep your date within the law and always in good taste!

Something New and Different

1. Mission Impossible: When your date comes to the door, he finds a tape recorder and an envelope with your picture in it. He will hear a taped message: "Good evening, Mr. _____. The picture you see before you is your date. Your mission, Mr. _____, should you decide to accept it, is to find her." (Elaborate on this.) Then send him all over with clues. Have people in trench coats to assist in his search. During this time, you can be watching from a safe observation point. When he finally finds you, have a candlelight dinner waiting.
2. Six people go to a drive-in restaurant. Don't take a car, but pretend you are in one. Position yourself as if in a car. "Drive" into a parking spot and order. Be very serious. When finished, back up and skid out of driveway.
3. Dress up in pioneer clothes. Take a box lunch and go to visit old trains.
4. Dress up in old-fashioned clothes, and go to an old-fashioned ice cream store.
5. Blindfold your date and drive around until she is lost. End on the top terrace of a parking lot overlooking the lights of the city.
6. Pack a lot of people in a small car and go buy one small drink with lots of straws.
7. Go shopping and see who can find the weirdest and cheapest item for the other person.
8. Bake cakes; decorate them blindfolded, with spatulas.
9. Have a fingerpainting party—with toes.
10. If you don't ski, dress up like a ski pro and spend the day at a ski lodge.
11. Paint the icicles hanging from rocks in the canyons or on your house.
12. Grab a book—climb a tree and read together.
13. Have a whipped cream fight (with pressure cans).
14. Draw pictures of each other.
15. Go pumpkin caroling or carving.
16. Go to a visitors center or museum and pretend your date is the guide.
17. Go for a midnight hike on snowshoes.

18. Have a mud-bowl game: play football or soccer in the mud and go swimming afterwards to clean off.
19. Go shopping and pretend you are married.
20. Park in a secluded place and listen to "Mystery Theater" radio drama or other old programs on the radio.
21. Have a backwards party: do everything backwards (klaw, klat, sserd, tae, .cte)
22. Take a survey that you made up, asking such questions as:

    a. How many times do you brush your teeth?
    b. How many thumbs do you have on your left hand?
    c. What did you have for dinner?
    d. Who is on the school debate team?
23. Have a party in the back of a rented moving van that has been fixed up with paper on the walls, pictures, and furniture. Have food and dancing.
24. Go Christmas caroling down Main Street in July.
25. Dress up like Mr. and Mrs. Santa Claus and go to a dance in June.
26. Make a mural on butcher paper.
27. Rent a bus. Girls ask boys but don't tell anything about it. Meet and board the bus. Drive to another city and go roller skating. On the return trip eat dinners that the girls made previously and have a bib-making contest.
28. Style your girl/boy friend's hair—put her makeup on for her.
29. Cut out pictures from a magazine to tell your life story, or make up a story from them.
30. Long distance dinner: You and a friend who lives far away decide on menu and exact time to eat, then pretend you are eating together.
31. Have a picnic on a golf course and then play golf.
32. Hunt for four-leaf clovers and make the wishes come true.
33. Walk through the city and see how many people you can talk to.
34. Take instant camera pictures of people and give the pictures to them.
35. Have a children's song sing-along.
36. Build a raft and use it.

37. Pan for gold.
38. Buy a coloring book; go to an ice cream store and color while eating ice cream. Have a stranger judge your work.
39. Dress up like a gangster and kidnap your date gangster-style in an old car. Blindfold her and take her to a cabin for dinner and old movies.
40. Have a cheerleader tryout; make up cheers and routines.
41. Skateboard in the evening in a deserted parking lot (get permission from the owner first).
4?. Have a treasure hunt, but collect photographs instead of objects.
43. Drive out to the desert and arrange rocks to make words.
44. "Kidnap" your parents and take them to dinner.
45. Have a bubble-blowing contest with bubble gum or soap bubbles.
46. Dress up in boxes and paint each other's box.
47. Instead of a car wash, have a dog wash to make money.
48. Wash stop signs.
49. Pick her up for the formal dance on horseback, in a limousine, semi-tractor, or other unusual vehicle.
50. Go to a Disney movie in a Disney costume.
51. Go bowling in formal attire.
52. Show old movies at the "drive-in" (an auto repair shop). Serve popcorn.
53. Have a "Pirates of the Caribbean" party (especially good at the beach or sand dunes). Invitations are written in old English script and sent in bottles. Have a hidden treasure map (put clues in bottles). The treasure can be toy jewelry or a picnic lunch.
54. Arrange this one beforehand with a theater owner. Invite your date to the theater. When you get there, the theater will be closed but you put on a play complete with tickets and programs. Use toys for props.
55. Have a blindfold dance.
56. Have a sound scavenger hunt. Make a tape recording of unusual sounds.
57. Have a compass hike—give only compass direction and the number of steps in each direction.
58. Send your date an anonymous reserved seat ticket to

some event, and when she arrives she sits down next to you.

59. Climb a flagpole.
60. Have yourself delivered to your date in a box.
61. Bigger and Better Party: Start each of several groups with a small toy and have them go door to door asking to trade for something bigger or better. Give a prize for the group with the biggest or best article after one hour.
62. Play hide-and-seek, tag, or cops and robbers on horseback.
63. Go on a date where you don't spend more than $1.00. For example, you might buy birdseed to feed the birds in the park and marshmallows to roast over an open fire.
64. Go on an old man, old lady date. The girls sit in the back seat, boys in the front, girls sit together at the game, etc.
65. Be clowns in a parade.
66. Have a blindfold scavenger hunt. Find things that are wet, cold, hard, soft, made of wood, or plastic.
67. Have a shaving cream fight.
68. Play basketball in formal wear.
69. Go on a date where neither of you can communicate verbally.
70. Take her to a "drive-in movie" in a pasture: bring your own projector and screen or just show prints or look at a picture book and make up your own story.
71. Have a paper-airplane-flying contest. See who can make the most interesting and best-designed plane.
72. Play marbles at City Hall.
73. Dress up in a costume from another country and go to a movie.
74. Have a shoe-shining party.
75. Write a list of things to do on a date.
76. Take a roll of pennies to a shopping center, and make wishes in a wishing well.
77. Rent a covered wagon and horses. Dress up like pioneers, and go for a ride. Have a dinner of homemade bread, wild onions, and raw milk.
78. Go ghosting. Put on a white sheet and run around the neighborhood.
79. Bake some cookies and take them to the parking lot at-

tendant and ticket seller at a theater.

80. Buy a twelve-foot length of decorating plastic tubing. Tie one end and it becomes a bib sack. If you run with it, it will fill with air. Tie the other end and you have a giant balloon. Play keep-away or toss it in the air, not letting it touch the ground.
81. Look up little-used words, then make up your own definitions. With several couples make a game of it.
82. Show a movie from the public library in a storage shed or root cellar.
83. Go to the pool or beach in an old-fashioned swimsuit.
84. Wrap presents for older people and leave them on their doorsteps; ring the bell and run.
85. Find a place where there is an echo and have an instrumental and/or vocal jam session. The instruments may be improvised.
86. Have a scavenger hunt for cookie and cake ingredients and then go home and make them.
87. Have a tape-recording contest. See who can come up with the most unusual sounds.

Ah, Those Were the Days
88. Have a hula hoop contest.
89. Play five-step with a football: kick the ball back and forth. Each time you catch it you move five steps closer to the other person's goal. When you kick it over without your opponent's catching it, you score a point.
90. Play Red Rover, Red Rover, send _____ right over.
91. Play dolls, with tea service and doll house.
92. Run through the sprinklers.
93. Build a dam in the gutter on a rainy day and go wading.
94. Have a knot-tying contest. (If you don't remember how to tie knots, consult a Boy Scout handbook.)
95. Have a grass fight.
96. Listen to old radio shows.
97. Build a tree house.
98. Figure out some clever April Fool's pranks.
99. Ride a bicycle built for two.
100. Jump puddles in the rain.
101. Swim in an old-fashioned swimming hole.

102. Ride in a horse-drawn sleigh.
103. Go "bibbiting" (frog hunting).
104. Try walking on tin-can stilts.
105. Cut an old inner tube to make one long tube instead of a circle. Wire one end closed and the other end around a hose. Fill it with water and play on it.
106. Hopscotch.
107. Jump rope (with all the old jump-rope rhymes).
108. Marbles.
109. Cowboys and Indians.
110. Four Square.
111. Hide-and-seek (at the park).
112. Kick the Can.
113. Run, Sheepy, Run.
114. Fox and Geese.
115. Jacks.
116. No Bears Are Out Tonight.
117. Frozen Tag.
118. Statues.
119. Cops and Robbers.
120. Tiddlywinks. Have a tournament.
121. Jack-in-the-Bush. (Each person has 25 marbles. The first person holds up some marbles in one fist. The other person tries to guess how many there are, and he must give up the difference between the guess and the actual amount. Continue until one is out of marbles.)
122. Croquet. Play it on the desert, or by night with flashlights.
123. Foosball.
124. License plate games: Make up words from letters on license plates while driving around. Or find each letter of the alphabet, in succession, on license plates or billboards.
125. Chinese jump rope.
126. Paper dolls.
127. Toy trains.
128. Puzzles. Try making your own.
129. Coloring books.
130. Mud pies.
131. A sand pile.

132. Crayons and butcher paper.
133. Fingerpaints.
134. Origami—paper folding. Make planes, birds, etc.
135. Slot car races.
136. Spelling bees.
137. Clay-modeling.
138. Tricycles.
139. Pinewood Derby.
140. Have an all-night Ping-Pong tournament.
141. Watch "Sesame Street," "Mr. Rogers' Neighborhood," or Saturday cartoons on TV.
142. Go to a kids' matinee.
143. Write to Santa.
144. Read children's books. Visit the children's section of the library.
145. Frost graham crackers.
146. Make soap sculptures.
147. Weave baskets.
148. Sneak cookies from the cookie jar.
149. Build a model plane or car.
150. Cut dolls, snowflakes, or other things out of paper.
151. Build a clubhouse.
152. Collect deposit bottles to buy penny candy.
153. Play in an open fire hydrant (with permission) on a hot summer day.
154. Build a snowman.
155. Visit a department store Santa. Sit on his lap and tell him what you want for Christmas.

Fun With Sports
156. Cross-country ski.
157. Downhill ski.
158. Snow shoe.
159. Sleighride.
160. Sculpt in the snow.
161. Toboggan.
162. Play hockey.
163. Ice skate.
164. Hike to a cabin in winter with no snowshoes.
165. Go tubing.

166. Play a football game in the snow.
167. Golf in the snow with green or red balls.
168. Slide down an Alpine slide.
169. Snowmobile.
170. Ice block.
171. Spend an evening at the spa or sports facility.
172. Bobsled.
173. Watch birds.
174. Fly kites you made yourself.
175. Go hanggliding.
176. Have a tug-of-war over a creek.
177. Chase wild rabbits in a jeep.
178. Have a chariot race.
179. Play hole-in-one in the backyard.
180. Go go-cart racing.
181. Spend time at the gym—swim, exercise, play paddle-ball.
182. Attend a karate tournament; hold your own demonstration.
183. Have a gymnastics contest. Stand on your head, walk on your hands, turn cartwheels.
184. Arm wrestle, thumb wrestle, Indian leg wrestle.
185. Bowl.
186. Play racquetball or handball.
187. Roller skate.
188. Watch your date participate in an athletic event.
189. Go hot-air ballooning.
190. Run in a marathon. Getting in shape is half the fun.
191. Rent a gym and have all your friends over.
192. Play three-legged basketball.
193. Play donkey basketball.
194. Play "around the Ping-Pong table." Several people run around the table and hit the ball just once; when you miss you are out.
195. Lift weights.
196. Play broom hockey. (Played in a gym with brooms and an eraser for a puck.)
197. Play Frisbee football.
198. Play Frisbee golf.

199. Go moonlight sailing.
200. Have a Frisbee contest.
201. Have a Jell-O fight.
202. Play on a trampoline.
203. Parachute from a plane, or skydive.
204. Go golf ball hunting.
205. Swim.
206. Take a boat trip.
207. Glide in a sail plane.
208. Scuba dive.
209. Dig clams on the beach.
210. Canoe.
211. Sail.
212. Surf or body surf.
213. Play water basketball.
214. Go speedboat racing.
215. Run the river, go tubing.
216. Water-ski.
217. Go sand surfing.
218. Go sand jumping at the dunes.
219. Race dune buggies.
220. Drag race.
221. Bike ride. Try it at night.
222. Ride motorcycles.
223. Hunt (using rifles, bow and arrow, or muzzle loaders):

a. duck	d. antelope	g. mouse	j. rabbits
b. deer	e. moose	h. quail	
c. coyote	f. elk	i. dove	

224. Fish.
225. Backpack in a wilderness area.
226. Jog.
227. Trap shoot.
228. Target shoot.
229. Go to the driving range.
230. Go miniature golfing.
231. Play soccer.
232. Play tennis at night. Play doubles with Mom and Dad or little sister and brother.
233. Have a sports day: tennis and football, golf, bowling and skateboarding, etc.

234. Take family members to a ballgame.
235. Ride horses.
236. Hunt for grunion or cisco (types of fish).
237. Join a yacht race.
238. Umpire a Little League game.
239. Scuba dive in a public pool.
240. Go mountain climbing.
241. Go rock rappelling.
242. Play feather volleyball (blow feathers across the net).
243. Play balloon basketball or soccer or football.

In the Wild Blue Yonder
244. Gather pinenuts.
245. Fly glider planes.
246. Work in an archeological dig.
247. Visit Indian ruins.
248. Go early to a parade and fix breakfast and play games while you wait.
249. Skip stones on a lake.
250. Motorcycle in the rain.
251. Visit a water slide.
252. Dodge sprinklers on a golf course.
253. Have a helicopter drop you on top of a mountain and hike or ski down.
254. Rock slide in a waterfall.
255. Go on a nature hike.
256. Hike to a lake, build a raft, and float on it.
257. Have a treasure hunt in the canyon—clues may be hidden in trees or under rocks or use compass directions.
258. Eat a sunrise breakfast in the mountains or park.
259. Go to a wilderness area and learn what plants are edible and what they can be used for.
260. Go backpacking with several couples. Learn tolerance levels, interpersonal relationships skills, patience.
261. Hike to a waterfall and attempt to follow the feeding stream back to its original source.
262. Hunt for toadstools.
263. Take a geology field trip.
264. Take the tram to the top of a ski lift in the summer and hike down.

265. Rope swing in the mountains (make your own swing).
266. Pick berries.
267. Go snipe hunting.
268. Watch clouds—identify the shapes you see.
269. Bicycle to the park or canyon and have a picnic.
270. Go to the beach in the evening—swim, build a bonfire.
271. Build sand castles at the beach or park.
272. Go canoeing in the moonlight or have an early morning picnic in a canoe.
273. Have a costume party in the canyon.
274. Have an outdoor square dance.
275. Have an outdoor dinner and watch old-time movies outside.
276. Feed the ducks at a local park.
277. Picnic and frolic in a children's playground.
278. Go Christmas tree shopping or chopping. Decorate the tree with homemade decorations.
279. Build snow forts—have a snowball war.
280. Write messages in the snow.
281. Take a long ride or walk with your date and several little children.
282. Hunt fossils in the desert.
283. Go cave hunting or ghost hunting.
284. Have an old-fashioned hayride.
285. Take a tractor ride at a farm.
286. Visit a hog farm.
287. Have a star party—get several telescopes and locate constellations.
288. Go to a star-gazers' party sponsored by a planetarium.
289. Go for a drive with no destination in mind; stop at places that look interesting.
290. Have a water fight with hose, balloons, squirt guns, or in a pool or stream.
291. Visit an animal reserve.
292. Hunt shells on the beach.
293. Walk along the beach.
294. Hunt wild flowers. Buy a field guide to wild flowers.
295. Play lost. Have someone drop you off in the wilderness, and using a compass and map, find your way back.
296. Spend a "survival day" in the wilderness.

297. Visit a state or national park.
298. Go four-wheeling.
299. Have an Easter egg hunt.
300. Have a clambake.
301. Take your date on a bus ride locally or to another city.
302. Take a night flight in a private plane.
303. Play checkers in the park or on a rock in the mountains.
304. Visit a dam on a big river.
305. Hunt arrowheads.
306. Collect fall leaves and make an arrangement of them.
307. Take a walk in the rain; jump in the puddles.
308. Go horseback riding on the beach.
309. Go on a moonlight walk.
310. Try to catch a greased pig.
311. Take an early morning hike, watch the sunrise, and cook breakfast.
312. Go on a river cruise.
313. Go mushroom hunting.
314. Take a helicopter to a remote place for dinner (such as the desert or mountains).
315. Hunt night crawlers together.
316. Collect shore crabs using gum on a string or fishing line with bread.
317. Mow your initials in her lawn.
318. Play Frisbee baseball.
319. Count satellites.
320. Prepare some dishes from an outdoor cookbook.
321. Have a road rally where each partner navigates one half of the course and drives the other.
322. Go on a treasure hunt for wild flowers or rocks.
323. Catch butterflies and start a collection.
324. Catch insects and start a collection.

Doing the Town

325. Play computer games.
326. Watch passing cars. Each person chooses a color. See who can count the most cars in his color.
327. Cater a wedding.
328. Spend the night at a telethon.
329. Go bowling at midnight and then have breakfast.

UP-DATE

330. Go to a poetry reading at the library.
331. Pass out bubble gum on Main Street.
332. Watch TV at the airport.
333. Visit a cemetery. Look at old names and dates and make up stories about the people.
334. Buy some flowers. Go to town and give them away to different people.
335. Stop at each store in a shopping mall and, without revealing it to each other, pick your favorite item. Then see how you compare.
336. Act like a tourist in your own town.
337. Fly or drive to another town for dinner.
338. Run errands for the family.
339. Go on a date with a $2.00 limit.
340. Go to a tall building with an outside elevator and ride up and down.
341. Go to a movie in a small town and pretend you are from New York.
342. Ride a city bus for the whole route.
343. Have a cab, or a friend dressed as a chauffeur, pick up your date and deliver her to the destination.
344. Attend a missionary reunion, then go home and show mission slides.
345. Test-drive a snazzy foreign car.
346. Go to a garage or rummage sale.
347. Go to a bazaar.
348. Go to an amusement park.
349. Watch people and planes at the airport.
350. Go to a game arcade—see if you can beat her at Foosball or Ping-Pong.
351. Read magazines together at the public library.
352. Go to a drugstore and read the greeting cards. Buy one for her parents.
353. Go shopping for a family member.
354. Take a ferryboat ride and have a picnic.
355. Spend $1.00 at a thrift store.
356. Spend $1.00 at a swap meet.
357. Visit an old bookstore.
358. Visit a TV or movie studio.
359. Go to a barn dance.

92

360. Before a dance, go to a field and pick a corsage of wild flowers for your date.
361. Have a Spanish dance.
362. Go to a formal dance; then change into grubbies, and go bowling or on a picnic.
363. Go to a fancy charity ball.
364. Enjoy dancing and dinner at a swanky hotel.
365. Go furniture shopping in secondhand stores.
366. Go to another campus (where your team is playing) and stay with friends.
367. Play TV games in a department store.
368. Go to a store and play "The Price Is Right." Take turns guessing the prices of different items, and keep track of the differences. The person who guesses closest to the actual amount without going over gets a stick of bubble gum.
369. Watch a movie on videotape at the library.
370. Take a dinner cruise in a glass-bottomed boat.
371. Go to a zoo.
372. Attend a meeting of the city or town council.
373. Visit Temple Square.
374. Visit a unique shopping mall.
375. Visit historical sights.
376. Attend the prison follies at the state prison.
377. Visit the state capitol building.
378. Visit a museum.
379. Go to a "Parade of Homes."
380. Go to the Junior Prom in a dump truck.
381. Go to the rodeo or craft show at the state prison.
382. Visit a hospital or nursing home.
383. Visit the airport.
384. Visit a police station.
385. Go to a disco dance.
386. Visit a fire station.
387. Using a clipboard, go to a fair and act like a judge. Watch the people watch you.
388. Fly electronic model planes.
389. Visit travel agencies and plan a trip.
390. Visit a fish hatchery.
391. Go to a stock-car race.

392. Go to a rock concert.
393. Visit a laserium.
394. Go to a summer theater.
395. Visit an aquarium.
396. Visit a bird refuge or aviary.
397. Visit a museum of science and industry or natural history.
398. Visit art galleries.
399. Have an old-fashioned southern plantation ball.
400. Visit a humane shelter.
401. Consult the yellow pages for other places to visit.
402. Attend a ballet.
403. Attend a symphony concert.
404. Attend a theater production.
405. Attend the live concert of a performer.
406. Attend the opera.
407. Attend the circus.
408. Go to a rodeo.
409. Attend an ice show.
410. Go to the state fair.
411. Go to a planetarium.
412. Go to a dog or cat show.
413. Go to a horse show.
414. Go to a demolition derby.
415. Attend any exhibit that comes to your town and is open to the public, such as a car show, boat show, food show, hobby show, art show, jewelry show, photography show, sporting show, survival show, home repair show, antique show.
416. Attend a session of the legislature.
417. Attend a political convention, or any convention that comes to town.

After making prior arrangements:
418. Visit a Federal Reserve bank.
419. Visit a radio station.
420. Visit a mine (gold, silver, copper).
421. Visit a water treatment plant.
422. Visit a law firm.
423. Tour a newspaper or other printing plant.

424. Visit a milk-processing plant.
425. Visit a bakery.
426. Visit an animal hospital.
427. Visit a sewage-processing plant.

When the Car Breaks Down

428. Buy a model car or plane kit and assemble it.
429. Have a two-person pool, billiards, or Ping-Pong tournament.
430. Color Easter eggs for Christmas, Thanksgiving, the Fourth of July, or whatever holiday is coming up.
431. Find a candy recipe. Go to the store and buy ingredients. Make it together. (See how you share and work with one another.)
432. Have a dance lab—learn "Swan Lake."
433. Play charades.
434. Work crossword, dot-to-dot, and hidden word puzzles.
435. Play TV games:
    a. Concentration
    b. Password
    c. The Price Is Right
    d. Hollywood Squares
    e. Let's Make a Deal
    f. The $20,000 Pyramid
    g. Jeopardy
    h. Twenty Questions
    i. Family Feud
436. Play games with your date's family:
    a. Monopoly
    b. Pit
    c. Battleship
    d. Cootie
    e. Scrabble
    f. Yahtzee
    g. Life
    h. Clue
    i. Payday
    j. Aggravation
    k. Masterpiece
    l. Boggle or Big Boggle
437. Play "To Tell the Truth": Each person passes in five funny but true experiences. Head person chooses three people it could have happened to (including the real one, of course). Each of the three gives his version of the story. Group tries to identify the truth teller.
438. Have a Sadie Hawkins party/dance.

439. Have a square dance.
440. Have a smile contest.
441. Have a pet show.
442. Make up captions for pictures in family albums.
443. Read the newspaper together—including the comics.
444. Read the want-ads section of paper. Have each person choose his favorite item under each heading, and compare your choices.
445. Shop for week's groceries at home using newspaper ads.
446. Watch cultural presentations on public television.
447. Look up and learn unusual words in a dictionary.
448. With a small group, discuss current events.
449. Read a book together and discuss it.
450. Read the scriptures together.
451. Present a "Gong Show."
452. Learn magic tricks—give a magic show for the younger brothers and sisters.
453. Play electronic TV games.
454. Put on a slide show of your date when he or she was little.
455. Have a baby picture contest.
456. Cut advertisements out of magazines; hide the products or brand names and see if you can guess what is being advertised.
457. Go through a junk drawer together.
458. Explore your grandparents' attic or basement for hidden treasures.
459. Read your grandparents' or other ancestors' journals.
460. Play the piano and sing together.
461. Watch sports on TV or maybe a parade.
462. Watch the late movie on TV.
463. Knights of the Round Table: Discuss world events or brainstorm solutions for some problem.
464. Prepare a Sunday School lesson together.
465. Work on a church welfare project.
466. Help a farmer bed his turkeys or milk the cows.
467. Go to a marsh and collect water samples for biology.
468. Cut logs for firewood.
469. Plant a tree.
470. Share your goals for this month, year, life.

471. Go through a catalog and make selections from each section or page. Learn about each other's tastes.
472. Pick a historical person or period and read about the subject together.
473. Go to a lecture and then discuss it.
474. Pantomime your favorite songs.
475. Have a popcorn sculpting contest.
476. Have an ice sculpting contest.
477. If you date a schoolteacher, help correct tests or make a bulletin board.
478. Pretend to be an interior decorator and plan the redecoration of your home.
479. Design your dream house.
480. Make up costumes from old clothes.
481. Put notes in balloons suggesting things to do like sing favorite song, recite a commercial, or dance.
482. Bake notes into cookies.
483. Decorate your date's room.
484. Read a good church book, such as *A Marvelous Work and a Wonder*.
485. Have a root beer chug-a-lug contest.
486. Have a tall-tale contest, with the winner receiving a big fish.
487. Have a formal dinner followed by a Rook tournament.
488. Newspaper game: Cut up and repaste a newspaper so it will say something about your date. Or write a newspaper article about your date.
489. Rewrite the newspaper. Cut up articles and put together to make new headlines and stories.
490. Spend a quiet evening in front of the fireplace.
491. Start or work on your file system together.
492. Exchange white elephants.
493. Show slides of vacations, missions, or world-wide adventure.

The Way to a Young Man's Heart
494. Have a dress-up candlelight dinner complete with waiters and violins. You may need to use friends as the doorman, waiter, chauffeur, violinist, etc. Serve hamburgers, cereal, or TV dinners. If you cannot afford

much, try tuna fish sandwiches and use a flashlight instead of candles.

Use your own imagination in having dinners in the following places (be sure to get permission from the owner of the property on which you wish to have your party):
495. In a tent.
496. At McDonald's (in formal attire).
497. In the mountains or on top of a mountain or hill.
498. In the back of a pickup truck at a drive-in.
499. In a moving van.
500. On a card table in your school parking lot.
501. At a yacht club (a boat parked in a friend's garage). This one is especially fun after water-skiing.
502. In a barn—serve fried chicken.
503. In a tent in your own backyard.
504. In a semitrailer.
505. On a "deserted island" (in the middle of a river).
506. On a golf course in the snow.
507. On an inner tube in a swimming pool.
508. On top of (or under) a waterfall. Wear swimsuits.
509. In a tree or treehouse.
510. On a snow-covered mountain.
511. Under a giant tree.
512. In the furnace room.
513. In a decorated, large appliance box.
514. In an empty swimming pool.
515. On a raft.
516. Have a progressive dinner.
517. Have a canyon cookout—tin-foil dinner.
518. Dress up in a formal attire to eat freeze-dried food.
519. Have a fondue party.
520. Have a luau.
521. Have a corn roast.
522. Have a backyard barbeque and lawn games.
523. Try waffles with lots of different toppings.
524. Fix a meal for your date's parents.
525. Surprise your date with dinner cooked by some of your friends—complete with candlelight and romantic music.
526. Have an international dinner.

Bake notes in the dishes telling your date what to eat next.

527. Have a surprise birthday or anniversary dinner for the parents of you or your date.
528. Have dinner catered on the top floor of a skyscraper.
529. Have dinner at a hospital snack bar.
530. Have a Chinese dinner, with chopsticks and fortune cookies. Sit on floor.
531. Have a progressive dinner with a group of friends. A different course is served at each home.
532. Take your date to the "pitside" restaurant and on an airplane ride.
533. Have a hobo dinner: cook everything in one pot and eat out of empty tin cans.
534. Choose a time-period (such as 1950s or Gay Nineties), and dress appropriately for dinner.
535. Take the train to another city, eat dinner, and drive home (take your car there in advance).
536. Have dinner while watching a tennis match.
537. Get up early (3:00 or 4:00 a.m.) for breakfast at home or at an all-night restaurant.
538. Select five or six different hamburger stands—buy one item at each place and end up at a park to eat it. (Try this as a race between teams.)
539. Have a mixed-up dinner: menu in riddles, food in strange sizes and colors.
540. Have a group dinner: Each person brings his favorite food. Don't tell what it is but have a rhyme about it. The clues are drawn out of a hat. The group guesses what it is. Eat the items in the order they are drawn.
541. Have a reverse dinner. Start with the dessert and work backwards.
542. Pots and pans dinner: Use a newspaper tablecloth, pans and spatulas instead of plates and utensils, vases for cups, funny bibs. Serve something difficult to eat.
543. Prepare a gourmet dinner together.
544. Have a numbers dinner. Each item is represented by only a number on a menu. The order of the dinner is determined by the order in which numbers are chosen.
545. Have a progressive dinner party, but go to restaurants for each course.
546. Prepare dishes from a different country and dress up in costumes typical of that country.

547. Have a picnic in a canyon or on the beach.
548. Make a menu of what you are going to feed your date, but give the items strange names.
549. Pick strawberries or other fruit and eat it with home-made ice cream.
550. Have a taco bust.
551. Invite several couples to bring their favorite recipes and prepare them together.
552. Have lunch at a hospital cafeteria and visit with the patients.
553. Have a picnic lunch raffle. Eat with the girl whose lunch you buy.
554. Go to a health food store and sample the food.
555. Have a potluck dinner party.
556. Have a "Come as You Are" dinner party. Call other couples at dinnertime the night before the party. Have them come dressed as they were when they were called and also bring something they were eating.
557. The "what shall we eat after the date" syndrome, or if you're tired of hamburgers and too poor for steak, try:
taffy
apple pie
cakes
ice cream
homemade bread
peanut butter and jam sandwiches
roast beef sandwiches
pizza (make your own)
popcorn
salad bar
small sandwiches
tacos
watermelon
fruit kabobs
hot chocolate and toast or donuts
waffles with ice cream and fruit topping
s'mores (melt marshmallows over stove burner)
cookies (have a contest frosting them)
variety of cold cereal—have you tried Wheaties?
scrambled egg sandwiches

100

scones (use frozen bread/roll dough)
cold chicken and potato salad
chili
cider and donuts
punch and cookies
cheese and crackers
relish plate
banana splits
cheese soup and bread sticks
omelettes
green eggs and ham
cold cuts
crepes
breaded chicken (chicken sandwich)
vegetable soup
quiche
fondue (cheese, bread, meat, chocolate with bananas or marshmallows)
tempura batter with fresh vegetables and fish
make your own sandwiches (have a variety of breads, cold cuts, cheeses)

558. Have a salmon fry.
559. Go on a safari: set up a tent in your front room with all the plants you can find.
560. Ancestor potluck: Each person brings a dish from the country where his or her ancestors were born.
561. Have a dinner with all the food and decorations the same color.
562. For those watching their weight, create a low-calorie meal.
563. Have dinner in a field and eat pork and beans from a can.
564. Have a pizza-decorating contest.
565. Have a vegetarian party.
566. Prepare a Passover feast (consult your Jewish friends).
567. Roast marshmallows on toothpicks over a candle.
568. Prepare banana splits. Have a contest to see who can be the most creative.
569. Pick fruit—cherries, apples, peaches—and make a pie.
570. Try role reversal—let him clean up the dishes while she reads the paper and relaxes.

571. Help your parents prepare Thanksgiving dinner.
572. Have a western dinner, with beef stew and biscuits. Prepare a mess kit for each guest: wooden spoon, canteens, bandanas for napkins.
573. Have a miniature dinner on doll dishes (Cornish game hen, little gelatin molds, birthday candles for centerpiece, little pies).
574. Have a Renaissance dinner: grape juice, homemade bread and cheese, no utensils.
575. Go to the supermarket and give each one a dollar or two. Each person buys his favorite food without letting the others know what it is. Take it home and share it.

Can a Girl with Paint on Her Nose Find Happiness with a Boy Mechanic?

576. Go to a farm and help with the chores.
577. Plant a garden.
578. Harvest food together and can it.
579. Plant and care for flowers
580. Do yard work (mow lawn, rake leaves, weed garden, shovel walks).
581. Rake up autumn leaves and bury each other in them.
582. Paint addresses on curbs—earn some money.
583. Paint house trim.
584. Reshingle a roof.
585. Help with a decorating project, such as wallpapering or painting.
586. Move furniture.
587. Do ironing together.
588. Scrub and wax floor.
589. Vacuum, dust.
590. Paint the car.
591. Tune an automobile engine; change oil.
592. Wash and wax the car, have a water fight.
593. Change regular tires to snow tires or vice versa.
594. Clean out his glove compartment—amazing what you will learn about him.
595. Refinish furniture.
596. Take a reupholstering or furniture-building class together, or any other kind of class.

597. Go to junk stores, find something unusual and fix it up.
598. Build something together, maybe a lasting relationship.
599. Put together an ant farm.
600. Fix a broken TV or radio.
601. Do homework together.
602. Keep a scrapbook or a journal of your activities together.
603. Build a crystal radio.
604. Landscape a yard.
605. Do the wash in a laundromat.
606. Work together on a research paper.
607. Usher at a symphony or other civic event.
608. Build a car from a kit.
609. Build a grandfather clock from a kit.
610. Train a dog.
611. Break a horse.
612. Build a water bed.
613. Repair a bike.

Is That You Singing, or Is My Cat Trying to Get In?

614. Learn a new talent or craft at a hobby shop.
615. Make a terrarium.
616. Make candles.
617. Make holiday decorations.
618. Make valentines.
619. Make paper airplanes or kites—have a contest flying them.
620. Make puppets and put on a show.
621. Collect flowers or weeds, dry and make your own arrangements.
622. Rock hunting—paint them or make funny creatures out of them.
623. Create a homemade band—each person has to make up an instrument.
624. Create your own opera.
625. Put on a play.
626. Make your own movie—sets, scripts, and sound. Give awards.
627. Find artistic settings for photos, painting, or just admiring.
628. Develop film in a darkroom.

UP-DATE

629. Make your own Halloween haunted house.
630. Do some pumpkin decorating—take finished product to someone.
631. "Teach date how to . . ." Find something you could teach your date and vice versa, do it, and see how well each relates to the skills and directions of the other.
632. Teach date to fox trot, tango, swing, jive, etc.
633. Switch roles: boys learn to make bread, girls learn to fix car.
634. Create a new food recipe.
635. Have a story-writing contest.
636. Latch hook a rug together.
637. Sew matching shirts.
638. Make a piece of furniture.
639. Make pottery.
640. Do macrame or a string design.
641. Make a collage.
642. Make mobiles.
643. Do fly-tying.
644. Have a reader's theater.
645. Paint by number.
646. Go to an old folks' dance—remember the fox trot and waltz?
647. Take a disco dance class.
648. Build and fly a gas model airplane.
649. Make and fly an electronic airplane.
650. Write music together.
651. Make up a modern dance.
652. Write a short story for the *New Era*.
653. Write poetry together—alternate lines or phrases.
654. Make posters together for an activity one or the other is involved with.
655. Try some musical duets.
656. Have a talent program, pillow concert.
657. Go to a date's house, listen to him/her practice a musical specialty.
658. Work on hobbies together.
659. Decorate garbage cans—a beautification project.
660. Make up a fairy tale, act it out, take slides to show on the next date, and give out acting awards (like bubble gum).

Do unto Others

661. Participate in a service or welfare project, such as canning or helping on stake farm.
662. Join a committee together and become involved.
663. Prepare Easter baskets to take to a hospital.
664. Play Easter Bunny for grown-up friends.
665. Sub for Santa.
666. Go to the zoo and take little children or retarded folk.
667. Go to a children's hospital and visit and play with the children.
668. Read to people in a nursing home.
669. Give a fireside for shut-ins.
670. Make get-well cards and deliver them.
671. Go to the store and buy colorful vegetables. Make a vegetable plate and secretly deliver it to someone who is sick.
672. Help with a fund-raising campaign.
673. Help gather and chop firewood for the Scouts' firewood drive.
674. Tutor: children, fellow students, your date.
675. Assist in anti-litterbug campaign.
676. Read for a blind person.
677. Clean up the yard and take the mess to the city dump in a pickup truck.
678. Have a work day. Help an elderly person paint the house or fence. Have a potluck dinner afterwards.
679. Throw a cleaning party—clothes, car, room— for someone else.
680. Help date with laundry.
681. Lend a hand, arm, and body to someone who is moving or redecorating.
682. Help with office jobs for one of parents.
683. Babysit kids of relatives or friends.
684. Take kids to a movie—buy them snacks.
685. Take brother and/or sister to see Santa or a parade.
686. Stuff envelopes for your favorite charity or political campaign.
687. Clean up someone's garage.
688. Go to a park and talk to the old people.
689. Clean up newly built homes.

690. Wash windows for the elderly.
691. Clean and trim the flower beds at the church.
692. Chaperone the sixth grade dance.
693 Put on a magic show for a child's birthday party.
694. Take someone a "for-no-reason-at-all" surprise.
695. Help a new mother:
    a. be a one-week diaper service.
    b. take dinner to the family.
    c. run to the store for her.
    d. take the other kids for an afternoon.
696. Take a new neighbor a "welcome-to-the-neighborhood" packet.
697. Go caroling to a healthy person, to a new neighbor, to someone sick or old.
698. Help a child prepare a talk for Primary.
699. Take a child to the cry room so the parents can sit through one entire meeting.
700. Visit an old friend or relative you haven't seen in ages.
701. Write a congratulatory note to someone who gave a talk or sang a song.
702. Support people in their endeavors by attending a play, recital, competition, or demonstration in which they participate.
703. Wash all cars in the neighborhood.
704. Help a grandparent do work—then have him/her tell about the good old days.
705. Take a widow with you to dinner and a play.
706. Give the dog a bath in the bathtub.
707. Adopt a grandparent or a shut-in; read, write for them, talk to them, help with the house or yard work.
708. Decorate a Christmas tree along with old folks.
709. Spend an afternoon helping the retarded.
710. Work on a political campaign.
711. Give blood.
712. Work on a campaign for cancer, M.S., March of Dimes, etc.
713. Help with Boy Scouts or Girl Scouts.
714. Go to the mountains and pick up trash.
715. Collect newspaper or cans.
716. Get acquainted with a neighbor you don't know.

Only on Sunday

717. Look at old family picture albums, scrapbooks, Book of Remembrance, Treasures of Truth.
718. Take an autumn afternoon walk through leaves.
719. Take a long ride.
720. Sit beside a quiet stream and talk about goals.
721. Quietly observe the sunrise or experience the sunset.
722. Write letters to missionaries, friends, or family.
723. Spend time with other person's family, participating in family activities.
724. Show home movies or slides of each person's childhood.
725. Go as a group to a cabin to listen to a Tabernacle Choir broadcast.
726. Play musical instruments, sing.
727. Read a play together.
728. Walk the dog.
729. Work on genealogy.
730. Attend a fireside.
731. Write your autobiography.
732. Participate in a religious study group.
733. Visit grandparents. Take a tape recorder and ask them to tell you about their dating years. Look at all of the old things they have collected.
734. Visit the sick.
735. Visit the lonely, the aged.
736. Discuss religion.
737. Attend church together.
738. Go to the temple grounds.
739. Go to a meeting where date participates.
740. Study scriptures together.
741. Listen to general conference.
742. Attend or listen to the Mormon Tabernacle Choir broadcast.
743. Make a presentation of a favorite poem, song, or book and tell why it is a favorite.
744. Have a sing-in on Sunday night—bring guitar, kazoo, etc.
745. Take a nature walk.
746. Take a walk through the snow.

UP-DATE
Families Make the Difference
747. Spend time doing almost anything with his/her family. (Any of the dates in this book could include family members.)
748. Double with your parents.
749. Go on a vacation with date's family.
750. Go to a family reunion.
751. Go to a family religious service (baptism, blessing, etc.).
752. Work in the yard with the family.
753. Spend a holiday with date's family.
754. Take your parents on a date.
755. Tend the little brothers and sisters.
756. Prepare a meal for both sets of parents.
757. Have a backyard party with date's parents.
758. Watch home movies.
759. Look at family photo albums.
760. Picket your home for higher allowance.
761. Attend family home evening at date's home.
762. Check out insurance policies.
763. Make up a budget as though you were married.
764. Shop together (even if you don't buy) for food, homes, cars, furniture, appliances, clothes.
765. Work at a business together (try a lemonade stand).
766. Prepare your income taxes together.

Index

Activities, family,
  questionnaire, 44-46
Adaptability and maturity, 26

Behavior, changing your own,
  in negotiation, 63
Boys: how to treat, 52; getting,
  to notice you, 70-71
"Briber," 19
"Bully," 19

Car: helping girl into, 51;
  sitting next to date in, 52
Cash, have adequate, on
  date, 52
Commitment and maturity, 26
Communication: defined, 57;
  resolution phase, 57, 63-65;
  understanding phase, 57-63
Competitiveness in dating, 9-10
Compliments, 52
Concern for others, 48
Conversation habits, list
  of distasteful, 56
Courtesy, 51
Courtship, length of, 11-12

Dancing dates, inadequacy
  of, 5-6
Date: answering door for, 51;
  introducing to family, 51;
  taking home, 53; making
  feel important, 69-70

Dateability: rating, 69-76;
  quick personality checklist,
  71; rating test, 71-76
Dates: variety and quality of,
  important, 12; turning down,
  50; asking for, 50-51;
  accepting, 50-51; offering
  alternative, 51
Dating: for personal growth,
  6; for self-gratification, 6;
  competitiveness in, 9-10;
  too narrow range of people,
  12-13; stages of, 14-17; those
  you don't think will be good
  dates, 51
Dating system, inadequacies of,
  5-13
Dating years, making the most
  of, 4-5
"Daydreamer," 19
Decision-making, 64-65
Defensiveness in
  communication, 58-59
Depression, overcoming, 21
Disclosure not necessarily
  communication, 59
Diversion to relieve tension,
  65
Divorce rate, 4
Don'ts, in listening, list of, 63

"Emotional filter" and
  communication, 58

requires hard work, 4, 9;
dating stage, 16-17
Mature person, traits of, 24-27
Maturity defined, 23
Mind-set and communication,
58
Mistakes, growing from, 18, 21
Money, have adequate, on date,
52
Motives, awareness of, in
communication, 58
Movie dates, inadequacy of, 5-6

Negativeness: in dates, 21;
overcoming, 21
Negotiate, learning to, 63-65

One person, emotional
involvement with, 12-13
Optimism and maturity, 24
Others: concern for, 48; serving,
48-49; accepting, 62

Past injuries, don't bring up,
64-65
Patterns of response in
negotiation, 64
Perceptions, accuracy of, 61-62
Perfection on dates, don't
always expect, 20
Persistence, need for, 22
Personal growth: from dating,
18; areas of, 18
Personality: importance of, 28;
inventory, 28-30; developing
good, 30-31
Physical habits, list of
distasteful, 54
Physical love, 53
Pie story, 9
Plan, executing, 65
Playing games, 7-8
Playing the field, 12-13;

dating stage, 16; advantages
of, 16
Point of view and
communication, 58
Positive thinking, 20-21

Postponement of gratification
and maturity, 24
Pretending, 7-8
Price, paying, for successful
marriage, 8-9, 49
Problem-solving, 64-65

Realism and maturity, 25
Records in negotiating, 65
Relationship: developing
attributes for good, 47-49;
depends on communication,
59-60: three attributes of
good, 60
Relating well to other people
and maturity, 26-27
Rephrase to understand, 63
Respect, mutual, attribute or
good relationship, 60
Response patterns in
negotiation, 64
Responsibility: for life, 21-22;
for feelings, 21-22; and
maturity, 25; for actions, 49
Responsible person, traits of, 49
Resolution phase of
communication, 57, 63-65
Restaurant, etiquette at, 52
"Rich man," 19

Sacrifice: in negotiation, 63-64;
origin of word, 64
Self: real, showing to dates, 8;
total, improving, 9-10;
liking, in disclosure, 59
Self-confidence: and maturity,
24; on dates, 69